# ASIA BOND MONITOR
## JUNE 2023

ADB

ASIAN DEVELOPMENT BANK

© 2023 Asian Development Bank
6 ADB Avenue, Mandaluyong City, 1550 Metro Manila, Philippines
Tel +63 2 8632 4444; Fax +63 2 8636 2444
www.adb.org

Some rights reserved. Published in 2023.

ISBN 978-92-9270-190-1 (print); 978-92-9270-191-8 (electronic); 978-92-9270-192-5 (ebook)
ISSN 2219-1518 (print), 2219-1526 (electronic)
Publication Stock No. TCS230207-2
DOI: http://dx.doi.org/10.22617/TCS230207-2

Note:
ADB recognizes "China" as the People's Republic of China; "Hong Kong" as Hong Kong, China; "Korea" as the Republic of Korea; "Siam" as Thailand; "Vietnam" as Viet Nam; and "Russia" as the Russian Federation.

Cover design by Erickson Mercado.

# Contents

## Emerging East Asian Local Currency Bond Markets: A Regional Update

Executive Summary ........................................................................................................ *vi*

Developments in Regional Financial Conditions ........................................................ *1*

Bond Market Developments in the First Quarter of 2023 ........................................ *13*

Recent Developments in ASEAN+3 Sustainable Bond Markets ................................ *22*

Policy and Regulatory Developments ........................................................................ *25*

Climate Risk Awareness and Fund Trading of Individual Investors ........................ *28*

Market Summaries

    China, People's Republic of ................................................................................ *31*

    Hong Kong, China ................................................................................................ *33*

    Indonesia ................................................................................................................ *35*

    Korea, Republic of ................................................................................................ *37*

    Malaysia ................................................................................................................ *40*

    Philippines ............................................................................................................ *42*

    Singapore .............................................................................................................. *44*

    Thailand ................................................................................................................ *46*

    Viet Nam ................................................................................................................ *48*

# Emerging East Asian Local Currency Bond Markets: A Regional Update

# Executive Summary

## Recent Developments in Financial Conditions in Emerging East Asia

Financial conditions in emerging East Asia have remained stable amid uncertainty over the future monetary stance of the United States (US) Federal Reserve.[1] Between 1 March and 2 June, regional equity markets and currencies slightly weakened, while risk premiums narrowed overall. Local currency (LCY) bond yields declined as inflationary pressure eased and regional central banks moderated their monetary tightening pace. The banking sector turmoil in the US and Europe has had limited impact on regional financial markets thus far.

Concerns over financial stability and elevated inflation generated uncertainty over the Federal Reserve's future monetary stance. While markets expected a pause in rate hikes at the June Federal Open Market Committee meeting, uncertainties persist over future monetary policy actions. In addition, the US debt ceiling negotiations in May raised some market concerns but had minimal impact on regional financial conditions. Amid these uncertainties, equity markets in the region posted a 1.7% (simple average) and 3.0% (market-weighted average) decline during the review period. Currencies slightly weakened by 0.7% (simple average) and 2.4% (gross-domestic-product-weighted average) against the US dollar, while risk premiums, as proxied by credit default swap spreads, slightly narrowed by 4.1 basis points (bps) (simple average) and 7.3 bps (gross-domestic-product-weighted average).

Emerging East Asian LCY government bond yields fell in nearly all markets as inflation trended downward and regional central banks slowed their monetary tightening. Most central banks in the region have moderated the pace of rate hikes, posting a total increase of 225 bps from eight rate hikes across the region between 1 January and 2 June. This contrasts with a total increase of 850 bps from 19 rate hikes between 1 August and 31 December 2022. The State Bank of Vietnam was the first regional central bank that reversed its monetary policy in 2023 by lowering the key policy rate by 50 bps in April, May, and June. Between 1 March and 2 June, 2-year and 10-year bond yields across emerging East Asia fell by an average of 36 bps and 44 bps, respectively.

Between 1 March and 2 June, the equity markets of members of the Association of Southeast Asian Nations (ASEAN) recorded net capital outflows of USD1.7 billion. However, equity markets across the entire region recorded net capital inflows of USD5.5 billion, driven by USD3.8 billion of net inflows in the People's Republic of China (PRC) owing to its economic rebound and USD3.4 billion of net inflows in the Republic of Korea on easing foreign investor restrictions. Regional LCY bond markets posted net foreign inflows of USD3.2 billion in March–April, buoyed by net inflows in the Republic of Korea and ASEAN economies, while the PRC recorded net outflows of USD5.7 billion on less attractive yields resulting from its accommodative monetary stance.

Regional financial conditions may continue to be affected by heightened uncertainty over the future path of US monetary policy. Other uncertainties over the short term include various headwinds to the global economic outlook, inflation and monetary policies at the domestic level, heavier debt burdens, and decrease in asset values due to higher interest rates. Emerging East Asian markets need to monitor debt sustainability and financial stability in an era of higher interest rates. Climate-related risks will further affect pricing and valuations in the financial sector over the medium term.

## Recent Developments in Local Currency Bond Markets in Emerging East Asia

Emerging East Asian LCY bond market reached a size of USD23.8 trillion at the end of March, on growth of 2.2% quarter-on-quarter (q-o-q) in the first quarter (Q1)

---

[1] Emerging East Asia is defined to include member states of the Association of Southeast Asian Nations (ASEAN) plus the People's Republic of China; Hong Kong, China; and the Republic of Korea.

of 2023, up from 1.2% q-o-q in the fourth quarter (Q4) of 2022. Growth was largely driven by increased issuance from the public sector. Government bonds accounted for 61.9% of the region's outstanding LCY bonds at the end of March. The growth of government bonds inched up to 2.6% q-o-q in Q1 2023 from 2.0% q-o-q in Q4 2022. Corporate bonds, which accounted for 35.8% of regional LCY bonds outstanding at the end of March, posted modest growth of 1.6% q-o-q in Q1 2023 following a contraction of 0.1% q-o-q in Q4 2022. At the end of March, aggregate outstanding LCY bonds in ASEAN stood at USD2.1 trillion, accounting for 9.0% of emerging East Asian LCY bonds outstanding.

LCY bond issuance in emerging East Asia tallied USD2.3 trillion in Q1 2023, with growth rebounding to 6.2% q-o-q from a contraction of 6.1% q-o-q in Q4 2022. Government bonds, which accounted for 43.0% of the regional issuance total, climbed by 12.4% q-o-q in Q1 2023, reversing a decline of 9.4% q-o-q in Q4 2022, as a number of governments frontloaded issuance during the quarter. In contrast, corporate bond issuance continued to contract, but at a moderated pace of 1.2% q-o-q in Q1 2023 compared with 4.1% q-o-q in Q4 2022, partly driven by higher interest rates. Aggregate issuance in ASEAN economies reached USD511.9 billion, representing 21.9% of the region's issuance during the quarter.

Emerging East Asian government bonds outstanding and issuance remained concentrated in medium- to long-term tenors in Q1 2023. Treasuries with maturities of over 5 years accounted for 53.4% of regional LCY government bonds outstanding at the end of March, while the size-weighted average maturity of all LCY government bonds in emerging East Asia was 9.0 years. In terms of issuance, 57.7% of LCY Treasury bonds issued in Q1 2023 carried maturities of over 5 years, while the size-weighted average maturity of LCY government bonds issued in Q1 2023 was 6.9 years. Banks, insurance companies, and pension funds remained the largest investors of LCY government bonds in the region.

The sustainable bond market in ASEAN+3 reached a size of USD633.9 billion at the end of March.[2] As a region, ASEAN+3 accounted for 17.7% of global sustainable bonds outstanding, following only the European Union,

which accounted for 38.6% of the global total. However, sustainable bonds outstanding only comprised 1.8% of total bonds outstanding in ASEAN+3 economies at the end of March. The PRC, the Republic of Korea, and ASEAN markets accounted for 46.0%, 21.6%, and 7.8%, respectively, of ASEAN+3's sustainable bond market. ASEAN+3's aggregate sustainable bond issuance in Q1 2023 reached USD47.7 billion, contracting 13.8% q-o-q after posting 2.7% q-o-q growth in Q4 2022. Green bonds (75.4%), LCY financing (61.7%), and private sector issuance (67.9%) dominated regional sustainable bond issuance. During the quarter, 50.8% and 24.2% of ASEAN+3 sustainable bond issuance carried maturities of over 1 year to 3 years and over 3 years to 5 years, respectively. Sustainable bond issuance had a size-weighted average tenor of 5.8 years in Q1 2023.

## Special Section: Climate Risk Awareness and Fund Trading of Individual Investors

This edition of the *Asia Bond Monitor* presents a special section on how increased climate risk awareness can influence investors' trading decisions. The literature has found that institutional investors incorporate climate-related risks into their investment decisions due to both financial and nonfinancial motives. This study adds new evidence to the literature by understanding how individual investment decisions are shaped by awareness of climate risks. Current knowledge shows that governments' environmental commitments are likely to raise investors' climate risk awareness. This study thus uses the PRC's announcement of dual carbon targets as an exogenous shock that is expected to boost investors' climate risk awareness. Using individual investors' account-level trading data, the study finds that after the announcement of dual carbon targets, individual investors in the PRC significantly increased their purchase of environmental, social, and governance (ESG) mutual funds relative to non-ESG mutual funds. This study indicates that governments' climate commitments and policies can drive resource allocation, not only via incentives and regulation but also by shaping investors' risk appetite and investment behavior. Policies that effectively guide investment decisions can help to cost-efficiently mobilize capital toward ESG investments.

---

[2] ASEAN+3 is defined to include member states of the Association of Southeast Asian Nations (ASEAN) plus the People's Republic of China; Hong Kong, China; Japan; and the Republic of Korea.

# Developments in Regional Financial Conditions

**Bond yields in emerging East Asia declined amid easing inflationary pressure and the moderating pace of monetary tightening.**

From 1 March to 2 June 2023, bond yields in emerging East Asia mostly fell on easing inflationary pressure in the region and the slowing pace of monetary tightening in the United States (US) and across the region.[1] Financial conditions across the region remained stable amid uncertainty over the monetary policy path of the Federal Reserve. Regional equity markets and currencies slightly weakened, while risk premiums narrowed overall (**Table A**). The impact of banking sector turmoil in the US and Europe has been limited in emerging East Asian markets.

During the review period, long-term bond yields trended downward on easing inflationary pressure in both advanced economies and emerging east Asia. Since January, inflation has been trending downward globally on declining oil and food prices (**Figure A**). Most short-term bond yields also declined during the review period

as the pace of monetary tightening moderated in both advanced and regional economies (**Table B**). Most central banks in the region have moderated their pace of rate hikes, raising interest rates by a total of 225 basis points (bps) through eight rate hikes across the region between 1 January and 2 June. This contrasts with a total increase of 850 bps from 19 rate hikes between 1 August and 31 December 2022.

The Federal Reserve hiked the federal funds rate by 25 bps at both its 21–22 March and 2–3 May Federal Open Market Committee (FOMC) meetings, bringing the target range to 5.00%–5.25%. While the market largely anticipated a pause in rate hikes in June to mitigate financial risks, there is some lingering uncertainty regarding the possibility of another rate hike in June (**Figure B**). In the March FOMC meeting statement, the Federal Reserve indicated that "some additional policy firming may be appropriate." Following the release of the March Core Consumer Price Index in the US on 12 April, which inched up to 5.6% from 5.5% in February, Federal Reserve Governor Christopher Waller

**Table A: Changes in Financial Conditions in Major Advanced Economies and Select Emerging East Asian Markets from 1 March to 2 June 2023**

| | 2-Year Government Bond Yield (bps) | 10-Year Government Bond Yield (bps) | 5-Year Credit Default Swap Spread (bps) | Equity Index (%) | FX Rate (%) |
|---|---|---|---|---|---|
| **Major Advanced Economies** | | | | | |
| Germany | (40) | (40) | 0.02 | 4.9 | 0.4 |
| Japan | (4) | (9) | (7) | 10.2 | (2.7) |
| United States | (38) | (30) | – | 8.4 | – |
| **Select Emerging East Asian Markets** | | | | | |
| China, People's Rep. of | (29) | (20) | (8) | (2.5) | (3.2) |
| Hong Kong, China | (44) | (43) | – | (8.1) | 0.2 |
| Indonesia | (82) | (49) | (6) | (3.1) | 1.6 |
| Korea, Rep. of | (35) | (27) | (7) | 7.8 | 1.4 |
| Malaysia | (7) | (23) | (10) | (4.8) | (2.3) |
| Philippines | 23 | (48) | (6) | (1.4) | (1.6) |
| Singapore | (32) | (43) | – | (2.7) | (0.6) |
| Thailand | 23 | (8) | 5 | (5.5) | 0.7 |
| Viet Nam | (136) | (133) | 3 | 4.8 | 1.2 |

( ) = negative, – = not available, bps = basis points, FX = foreign exchange.
Note: A positive (negative) value for the FX rate indicates the appreciation (depreciation) of the local currency against the United States dollar.
Source: *AsianBondsOnline* calculations based on Bloomberg LP data.

---

[1] Emerging East Asia is defined to include member states of the Association of Southeast Asian Nations (ASEAN) plus the People's Republic of China; Hong Kong, China; and the Republic of Korea.

## Figure A: Inflation in Advanced and Select Emerging East Asian Economies

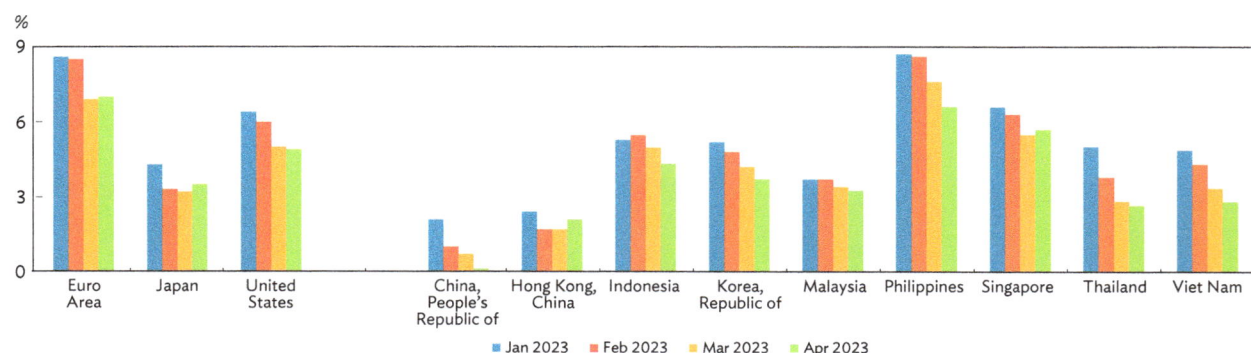

Note: Data coverage is from January to April 2023.
Sources: Various local sources.

## Table B: Changes in Monetary Stances in Major Advanced Economies and Select Emerging East Asian Markets

| Economy | Policy Rate 1-Jun-2022 (%) | Jun-2022 | Jul-2022 | Aug-2022 | Sep-2022 | Oct-2022 | Nov-2022 | Dec-2022 | Jan-2023 | Feb-2023 | Mar-2023 | Apr-2023 | May-2023 | Jun-2023 | Policy Rate 2-Jun-2023 (%) | Change in Policy Rates (basis points) |
|---|---|---|---|---|---|---|---|---|---|---|---|---|---|---|---|---|
| Euro Area | (0.50) | | ↑0.50 | | ↑0.75 | | ↑0.75 | ↑0.50 | | ↑0.50 | ↑0.50 | | ↑0.25 | | 3.25 | ↑375 |
| Japan | (0.10) | | | | | | | | | | | | | | (0.10) | |
| United Kingdom | 1.00 | ↑0.25 | | ↑0.50 | ↑0.50 | | ↑0.75 | ↑0.50 | | ↑0.50 | ↑0.25 | | ↑0.25 | | 4.50 | ↑350 |
| United States | 1.00 | ↑0.75 | ↑0.75 | | ↑0.75 | | ↑0.75 | ↑0.50 | | ↑0.25 | ↑0.25 | | ↑0.25 | | 5.25 | ↑425 |
| China, People's Rep. of | 2.85 | | | ↓0.10 | | | | | | | | | | | 2.75 | ↓10 |
| Indonesia | 3.50 | | | ↑0.25 | ↑0.50 | ↑0.50 | ↑0.50 | ↑0.25 | ↑0.25 | | | | | | 5.75 | ↑225 |
| Korea, Rep. of | 1.75 | | ↑0.50 | ↑0.25 | | ↑0.50 | ↑0.25 | | ↑0.25 | | | | | | 3.50 | ↑175 |
| Malaysia | 2.00 | | ↑0.25 | | ↑0.25 | | ↑0.25 | | | | | | ↑0.25 | | 3.00 | ↑100 |
| Philippines | 2.25 | ↑0.25 | ↑0.75 | ↑0.50 | ↑0.50 | | ↑0.75 | ↑0.50 | | ↑0.50 | ↑0.25 | | | | 6.25 | ↑400 |
| Singapore | – | | ↑ | | | ↑ | | | | | | | | | – | – |
| Thailand | 0.50 | | | ↑0.25 | ↑0.25 | | ↑0.25 | | ↑0.25 | | ↑0.25 | | ↑0.25 | | 2.00 | ↑150 |
| Viet Nam | 4.00 | | | | ↑1.00 | ↑1.00 | | | | | | ↓0.50 | ↓0.50 | | 5.00 | ↑100 |

( ) = negative.

Notes:
1. Data coverage is from 1 June 2022 to 2 June 2023.
2. For the People's Republic of China, data used in the chart are for the 1-year medium-term lending facility rate. While the 1-year benchmark lending rate is the official policy rate of the People's Bank of China, market players use the 1-year medium-term lending facility rate as a guide for the monetary policy direction of the People's Bank of China.
3. The up (down) arrow for Singapore signifies monetary policy tightening (loosening) by its central bank. The Monetary Authority of Singapore utilizes the Singapore dollar nominal effective exchange rate to guide its monetary policy.

Sources: Various central bank websites.

on 14 April emphasized that much still needs to be done on inflation. Nevertheless, the hawkish phrasing in the FOMC's March statement was removed from its May statement. Thus, the probability of a 25 bps rate hike in June fell from 16.6% on 14 April to zero after the FOMC meeting announcement on 4 May. On 10 May, Minneapolis Federal Reserve Bank President Neel Kashkari noted that inflation had been surprisingly stubborn and therefore tight monetary policy might need to be maintained for quite some time. On 12 May, Federal Reserve Governor Michelle Bowman indicated

that inflation remained high and further monetary tightening would be needed to lower inflation. On the same day, Chicago Federal Reserve Bank President Austan Goolsbee echoed that inflation remained too high. Meanwhile, the University of Michigan's survey of inflation expectations for the next 5–10 years rose to 3.2% in May 2023, marking a 12-year high. Comments by Federal Reserve Chairman Jerome Powell on 19 May that inflation was still too high led to an increase in the probability of a June rate hike from 10.7% on 11 May to as high as 66.6% on 30 May. The probability fell to 20.4%

**Figure B: Probability of a 25 bps Rate Hike at the Federal Open Market Committee Meeting on 13–14 June 2023**

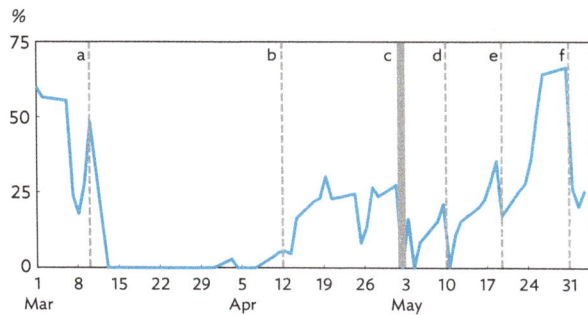

bps = basis points, FOMC = Federal Open Market Committee.

Note: Data are as of 2 June 2023.

a   Silicon Valley Bank placed under receivership.
b   March Core Consumer Price Index in the United States inched up to 5.6%.
c   FOMC May meeting.
d   Minneapolis Federal Reserve Bank President Neel Kashkari comments that tight monetary policy may be needed for an extended period.
e   Federal Reserve Chairman Jerome Powell noted that inflation is still too high.
f   Federal Reserve Governor Philip Jefferson speech indicated a pause in rate hike in the next FOMC meeting.

Source: CME FedWatch Tool (accessed on 3 June 2023).

on 1 June after comments by Federal Reserve Governor Philip Jefferson on 31 May that a pause in June would give time for policymakers to assess recent economic data.

Recent US economic data contributed to the mixed views regarding the potential pause in rate hikes by the Federal Reserve in June. Annualized gross domestic product (GDP) growth weakened to 1.3% in the first quarter (Q1) of 2023, based on a revised estimate, from 2.6% in the fourth quarter (Q4) of 2022. Consumer Price Index inflation continued to trend down to 4.9% year-on-year (y-o-y) in April from 5.0% y-o-y in March, 6.0% y-o-y in February, and 6.4% y-o-y in January. Meanwhile, the labor market remained strong, as nonfarm payrolls added 339,000 jobs in May from a revised 294,000 in April. Higher-than-expected nonfarm payrolls in May, released on 2 June, led a to a small rise in Federal Reserve rate hike probability to 25.3% on the same day. As widely expected, the Federal Reserve left its monetary policy unchanged at its 13–14 June FOMC meeting. Updated economic forecasts, however, indicate future rate hikes are still possible.

In the euro area, the European Central Bank (ECB) raised the policy rate by 25 bps on 4 May, which was smaller than the previous 50 bps rate hike on 16 March. This decision was partly influenced by the banking sector turmoil experienced in both the US and Europe in March. In the April Bank Lending Survey released on 2 May, the ECB

cited its concern over tightening bank lending, which was causing monetary growth to decline, as one reason for the smaller 25 bps rate hike. Both the 2-year and 10-year yields in Germany fell during the review period, largely driven by easing inflationary pressure and expectations that the ECB might adopt similar measures as the Federal Reserve to safeguard financial stability. While still elevated, inflation in the euro area continued to trend downward to 6.1% y-o-y in May from April (7.0%), March (6.9%), February (8.5%), and January (8.6%). Annualized GDP growth weakened to 1.0% in Q1 2023 from 1.8% in Q4 2022. However, the ECB emphasized that inflationary pressure remains unacceptably high. At the ECB's monetary policy press conference on 4 May, ECB President Christine Lagarde indicated that they "are not pausing." The ECB eventually raised its policy rate by 25 bps on 15 June.

Unlike in the US and euro area, the Bank of Japan (BOJ) left its easy monetary policy unchanged during the review period. However, in its 28 April monetary policy statement, the BOJ removed the phrase "it also expects short- and long-term policy interest rates to remain at their present or lower levels," replacing it with a plan to review existing monetary policy in 1–1.5 years. This led to some expectations that the BOJ might eventually adjust its easy monetary policy. The BOJ's updated economic forecasts in April showed a weakening GDP outlook and slightly higher inflation forecasts from those made in January. The GDP growth forecast was revised down to 1.4% from 1.7% for fiscal year 2023, but inflation forecasts were revised up to 1.8% from 1.6% for fiscal year 2023.

The 2-year and 10-year bond yields fell in nearly all emerging East Asian markets during the review period on declining inflation and the easing pace of monetary tightening among regional central banks. The largest decline in yields came from Viet Nam, which was the first regional central bank to reverse its monetary stance in 2023. The State Bank of Vietnam reduced its discount rate by 100 bps, effective 15 March, and reduced its key policy rate by 50 bps on both 3 April and 25 May to spur economic growth, after lower-than-expected GDP growth of 3.3% y-o-y in Q1 2023, and to support financial stability, especially in the real estate market. Since the start of 2022, Viet Nam's real estate equity index has fallen by more than half (**Figure C**). Amid weaknesses in Viet Nam's economy, the State Bank of Vietnam further reduced key policy rates by 50 bps, effective 19 June.

The Philippines and Thailand were the only two markets that saw an increase in the 2-year yield, due to relatively

**Figure C: Viet Nam Real Estate Equity Index**

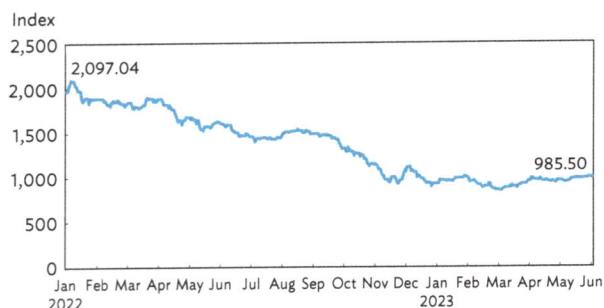

Index

2,097.04

985.50

Note: Data are as of 2 June 2023.
Source: Bloomberg LP.

**Figure D: Movements in Equity Indexes in Select Emerging East Asian Markets**

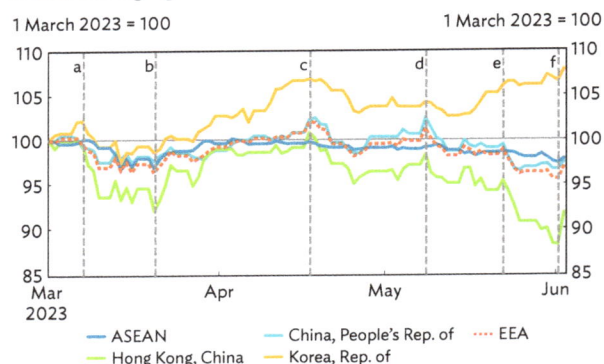

1 March 2023 = 100                    1 March 2023 = 100

ASEAN    China, People's Rep. of    EEA
Hong Kong, China    Korea, Rep. of

ASEAN = Association of Southeast Asian Nations, EEA = emerging East Asia, FOMC = Federal Open Market Committee, PRC = People's Republic of China, US = United States.

a   Chairman Powell's semi-annual report to Congress noted that interest rates will likely be higher-than-expected.
b   UBS takes control of Credit Suisse.
c   Weaker-than-expected investment and manufacturing data in the PRC.
d   US Treasury Secretary Yellen warns of consequences if debt ceiling is not raised.
e   Heightened market jitters over US debt ceiling negotiations, Japan announces additional technology export curbs to the PRC.
f   US Senate passes debt ceiling bill.

Notes:
1. ASEAN comprises the markets of Cambodia, Indonesia, the Lao People's Democratic Republic, Malaysia, the Philippines, Singapore, Thailand, and Viet Nam.
2. Data are as of 2 June 2023.

Source: *AsianBondsOnline* calculations based on Bloomberg LP data.

more aggressive monetary tightening since January 2023 compared with their regional peers (Table B). While inflation has been declining in the Philippines, it remained elevated at 6.6% y-o-y in April, the second highest across the region. The Bangko Sentral ng Pilipinas has raised policy rates twice for a cumulative total of 75 bps since the start of 2023. The Bank of Thailand raised the policy rate by 25 bps each in January, March, and May, as core inflation remained elevated. Thailand and the Philippines have tightened more than other regional central banks since the start of the year.

Uncertainties regarding ongoing US monetary tightening and headwinds to the regional economic outlook weighed on most emerging East Asian equity markets during the review period (**Figure D**). Between 1 March and 2 June, regional equity markets declined by 1.7% (simple average) and 3.0% (market-weighted). Weak economic data in the People's Republic of China (PRC) in April contributed to equity market losses in April and May. While the PRC's GDP growth accelerated to 4.5% y-o-y in Q1 2023 from 2.9% y-o-y in Q4 2022, April witnessed moderating industrial production and exports. Furthermore, both inflation and property investment have weakened in the PRC since January 2023.[2] The Republic of Korea posted a 7.8% gain in its equity market index during the review period, partly driven by portfolio inflows on easing foreign investor restrictions as the economy seeks inclusion in the Morgan Stanley Capital International Developed Market Index. Viet Nam's equity market rose by 4.8% during the same period on its easing monetary policy.

In May, negotiations over the debt ceiling in the US cast some uncertainty in global financial markets. US Treasury Secretary Janet Yellen warned on 1 May of the potential for the federal government to default on loan repayments by the first week of June if the debt ceiling was not raised. She later reiterated this on 7 May, citing that a failure to raise the debt ceiling could lead to "economic catastrophe." On 24 May, Fitch, one of the world's top credit rating agencies, placed the US' AAA long-term foreign-currency issuer default rating on "rating watch negative" over doubts that a debt ceiling deal would be negotiated in time. On 31 May, the US House of Representatives passed a bill to raise the government's borrowing limit and was followed by an approval in the Senate on 1 June. Despite the uncertainty around the US debt ceiling debate, it had minimal impacts on regional financial markets.

During the review period, emerging East Asian currencies generally weakened vis-à-vis the US dollar, with a slight depreciation of 0.7% (simple average) and 2.4% (GDP-weighted) (**Figure E**). In March, most regional currencies strengthened, following expectations of dovish monetary stances after Silicon Valley Bank was placed

---

[2] National Bureau of Statistics of China. 2023. "Investment in Real Estate Development for Jan-Apr." News release. 17 May. http://www.stats.gov.cn/english/PressRelease/202305/t20230519_1939833.html.

**Figure E: Changes in Select Emerging East Asian Currencies versus the United States Dollar**

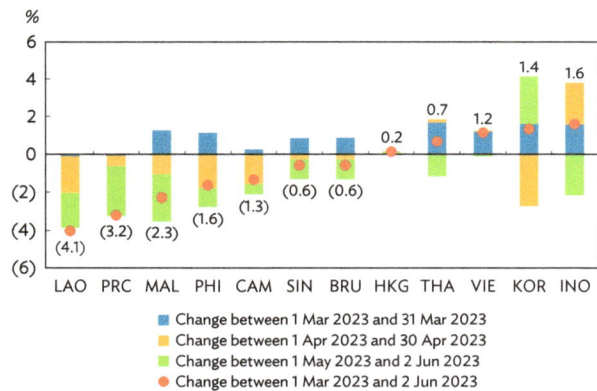

%

Change between 1 Mar 2023 and 31 Mar 2023
Change between 1 Apr 2023 and 30 Apr 2023
Change between 1 May 2023 and 2 Jun 2023
Change between 1 Mar 2023 and 2 Jun 2023

( ) = negative; BRU = Brunei Darussalam; CAM = Cambodia; HKG = Hong Kong, China; INO = Indonesia; KOR = Republic of Korea; LAO = Lao People's Democratic Republic; MAL = Malaysia; PHI = Philippines; PRC = People's Republic of China; SIN = Singapore; THA = Thailand; VIE = Viet Nam.

Notes:
1. A positive (negative) value for the foreign exchange rate indicates the appreciation (depreciation) of the local currency against the United States dollar.
2. The numbers above (below) each bar refer to the change between 1 March 2023 and 2 June 2023.

Source: *AsianBondsOnline* calculations based on Bloomberg LP data.

**Figure F: Changes in Credit Default Swap Spreads in Select Emerging East Asian Markets** (senior 5-year)

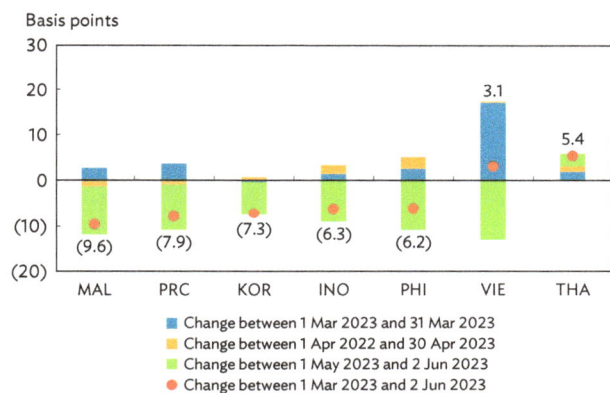

Basis points

Change between 1 Mar 2023 and 31 Mar 2023
Change between 1 Apr 2022 and 30 Apr 2023
Change between 1 May 2023 and 2 Jun 2023
Change between 1 Mar 2023 and 2 Jun 2023

( ) = negative; INO = Indonesia; KOR = Republic of Korea; MAL = Malaysia; PHI = Philippines; PRC = People's Republic of China; THA = Thailand; VIE = Viet Nam.

Note: The numbers above (below) each bar refer to the change in spreads between 1 March 2023 and 2 June 2023.

Source: *AsianBondsOnline* calculations based on Bloomberg LP data.

**Figure G: Capital Flows in Equity Markets in Emerging East Asia**

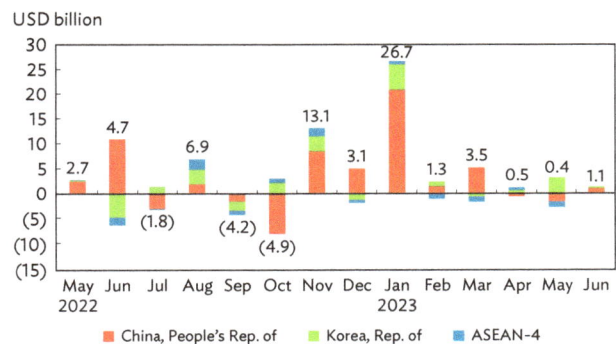

USD billion

China, People's Rep. of    Korea, Rep. of    ASEAN-4

( ) = outflows, USD = United States dollar.

Notes:
1. Data coverage is from 1 May 2022 to 2 June 2023.
2. The numbers above (below) each bar refer to net inflows (net outflows) for each month.
3. Emerging East Asia is defined to include member states of the Association of Southeast Asian Nations (ASEAN) plus the People's Republic of China; Hong Kong, China; and the Republic of Korea.
4. ASEAN-4 includes Indonesia, the Philippines, Thailand, and Viet Nam.

Source: Institute of International Finance.

under receivership on 10 March. The probability of a 50 bps rate hike by the Federal Reserve fell from 78.3% on 8 March to 40.2% on 10 March, then to zero on 13 March. However, in April and May, the US dollar strengthened again on signs of continued tightening. The biggest currency loss in emerging East Asia was recorded in the Lao People's Democratic Republic (Lao PDR) (4.1%) due to high inflation, a widening trade deficit, and debt stress.

Meanwhile, with expectations of a pause in rate hikes at the June FOMC meeting and a deal in place to raise the US debt ceiling, credit default swap (CDS) spreads, a typical measure of the risk premium, narrowed by 4.1 bps (simple average) and 7.3 bps (GDP-weighted) during the review period (**Figure F**). In contrast, CDS spreads in Thailand widened by 5 bps amid uncertainties following the general elections. In Viet Nam, CDS spreads widened 17.2 bps in March over liquidity concerns in the property sector and rising defaults in the corporate bond market. Based on a FiinRatings report, 69 issuers had failed to make payment on time as of 17 March, with a total default value amounting to VND94.3 trillion, 83.6% of which was from the real estate sector. Viet Nam's CDS spreads eventually rose by only a total of 3.0 bps between 1 March and 2 June. While the government eased corporate bond regulations in March, banks remained cautious in providing credit to the sector.

The region witnessed uneven capital flows into equity markets during the review period. There were USD5.5 billion of net inflows into emerging East Asian equity markets from 1 March to 2 June, driven primarily by net inflows in the PRC (USD3.8 billion) and the Republic of Korea (USD3.4 billion) (**Figure G**). The Association of Southeast Asian Nations (ASEAN) recorded net outflows of USD1.7 billion from 1 March to 2 June, with all ASEAN economies except Indonesia posting net outflows during the review period. Indonesia recorded net inflows of USD1.2 billion on the back of stable economic growth of 5.0% y-o-y in both Q1 2023 and Q4 2022. In the PRC, total net inflows of USD3.8 billion were buoyed by USD5.2 billion of net inflows in March after the PRC loosened visa restrictions on foreigners on 14 March. However, net outflows of USD0.7 billion in April and USD1.7 billion in May were recorded when weaker-than-expected economic data were released and the US announced plans to restrict investments in PRC technology companies. The Republic of Korea recorded monthly capital inflows in April and May over easing foreign investor restrictions as the economy seeks inclusion in the Morgan Stanley Capital International Developed Market Index.

On expectations of a more dovish monetary stance in the US resulting from turmoil in the banking sector, the region's local currency bond markets posted net foreign inflows of USD1.8 billion in March and USD1.5 billion in April, rebounding from net outflows of USD1.3 billion in January and USD11.2 billion in February (**Figure H**). ASEAN local currency bond markets recorded net inflows of USD3.2 billion in March–April.

During this 2-month period, Malaysia and Indonesia both recorded relatively large net inflows on declining inflation and a sound economic outlook, while Thailand posted marginal net inflows of USD0.3 billion due to uncertainty over the general election. The Philippines recorded net outflows of USD0.5 billion in March–April amid elevated inflation. The PRC recorded USD5.7 billion of net outflows in March–April as the accommodative monetary stance made the PRC's yields less attractive compared with those of other economies in the region. **Box 1** discusses the economic outlook for emerging East Asia in 2023.

Overall, financial conditions in emerging East Asia remained stable despite uncertainty over ongoing US monetary tightening and headwinds to the global economic outlook. Financial conditions were supported, however, by reduced inflationary pressure and moderated monetary tightening domestically. The regional financial system has remained resilient amid amplified financial risks from banking sector turmoil in the US and Europe. Asian banks are generally robust with limited direct exposure to banks in advanced economies with solvency issues. From 1 March to 2 June, the S&P Broad Market Index for Banks in Asia fell only 2.0%, compared with declines of 17.7% and 8.4% in the US and Europe, respectively (**Figure I**).

Nevertheless, there remain some key downside risks to the outlook for regional financial conditions. In the short term, uncertainty over the moderating pace of monetary

**Figure H: Foreign Capital Flows in Select Emerging East Asian Local Currency Bond Markets**

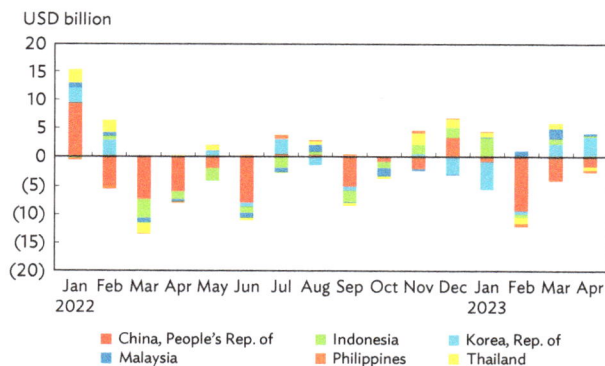

( ) = negative, USD = United States dollar.
Notes:
1. The Republic of Korea and Thailand provided data on bond flows. For the People's Republic of China, Indonesia, Malaysia, and the Philippines, month-on-month changes in foreign holdings of local currency government bonds were used as a proxy for bond flows.
2. Data are as of 30 April 2023.
3. Figures were computed based on 30 April 2023 exchange rates and do not include currency effects.

Sources: People's Republic of China (Bloomberg LP); Indonesia (Directorate General of Budget Financing and Risk Management, Ministry of Finance); Republic of Korea (Financial Supervisory Service); Malaysia (Bank Negara Malaysia); Philippines (Bureau of the Treasury); and Thailand (Thai Bond Market Association).

**Figure I: S&P Broad Market Indexes for Banking Stocks in Asia, Europe, and the United States**

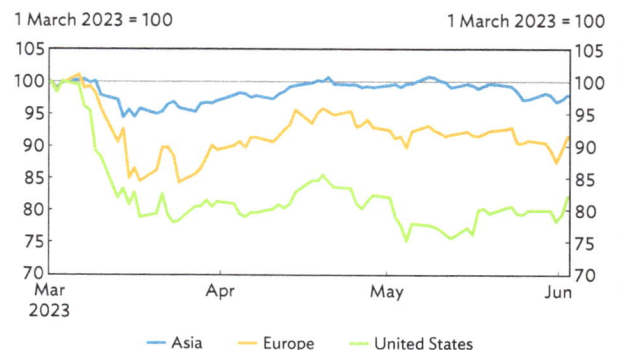

Notes:
1. Data are as of 2 June 2023.
2. S&P Global's Broad Market Indexes for banks are comprehensive benchmarks of bank stocks in Asia and the Pacific, Europe, and the United States, and are subindexes of the S&P Global BMI for Banks.

Source: S&P Global.

# Box 1: Economic Outlook in Developing Asia

Developing Asia's economies are reopening with dynamism.[a] There has been a revival of private consumption, investment, and services—including tourism—now that the coronavirus disease (COVID-19) pandemic seems to have largely passed. The outlook for the region is improving after economies showed resilience last year amid weakened demand from advanced economies, COVID-19 lockdowns in the People's Republic of China (PRC), monetary policy tightening, and the Russian invasion of Ukraine.

The PRC's reopening after last year's stringent lockdowns is brightening the outlook for both the region and the global economy, with growth in the PRC forecast to rebound to 5.0% this year and 4.5% in 2024. Household demand is expected to recover as COVID-19 restrictions are lifted. Continued fiscal spending, notably infrastructure investment, will help spur the economic recovery, particularly against a backdrop of weakening global demand. In the rest of East Asia, Hong Kong, China is forecast to bounce back with growth of 3.6% in 2023, supported by the PRC's reopening, after contracting by 3.5% in 2022. In contrast, growth will be weaker in the Republic of Korea, as exports of memory chips and consumer electronics have been hit hard by plunging global demand. On balance, growth in East Asia will accelerate from 2.8% in 2022 to 4.6% in 2023 before moderating to 4.2% in 2024 (**Table B1**).

In Southeast Asia, growth is moderating after a sharp rebound in 2022 as economies reopened. The subregion is expected to grow by 4.7% in 2023, down from 5.6% last year. Economies will continue reopening but tighter monetary conditions amid persistent inflation will dampen growth prospects. Weak exports will also drag down growth as demand from advanced economies continues to shift away from goods, particularly electronics, and back to services. Countries where tourism accounts for a large share of gross domestic product—notably Cambodia, the Philippines, and Thailand—will benefit from the return of tourists from the PRC. Viet Nam is forecast to grow the fastest in the subregion, 6.5% in 2023 and 6.8% in 2024, as tourism, public investment, and stimulus programs keep domestic consumption strong.

Overall, developing Asia's growth is expected to reach 4.8% both this year and in 2024, with South Asia, led by resilient growth in India, expected to grow faster than other subregions. Headline inflation in the region is gradually returning to pre-pandemic levels. Inflation in developing Asia is forecast at 4.2% this year and 3.3% in 2024, driven by muted inflation in the PRC. The decline in inflation will be supported by monetary tightening and easing supply chain and shipping bottlenecks.

The banking turmoil in Europe and the United States (US) is an indication that financial stability risks have heightened, especially since the overall effects of the crises in these economies remain uncertain. The effects of the banking turmoil on developing Asia have been limited so far as most Asian banks were not exposed to the failed US banks. Moreover, Asian banks are relatively healthy with higher capital buffers than their US counterparts and relatively low nonperforming loan ratios. Nevertheless, there are potential vulnerabilities in some regional economies with high credit risk, a poor institutional framework, or weak macroeconomic fundamentals. These fragilities should be monitored closely. More widespread banking sector turmoil, although a low-probability risk, could precipitate slower growth and financial instability, or even a financial crisis in the region. This would disproportionately affect more vulnerable groups, increase inequality and long-term unemployment, and cause persistent damage to the productive capacity of developing Asian economies.

Aside from increased financial stability risks, an array of immediate and emerging challenges could still hinder the region's recovery. Policy makers should stay vigilant with regard to higher interest rates and debt. Governments must continue supporting multilateralism and lean against the risks of global fracturing. And developing Asia must continue its strong regional cooperation to weather this uncertain environment.

**Table B1: Gross Domestic Product Growth and Inflation Forecasts** (% per year)

|  | GDP Growth | | | Inflation | | |
|---|---|---|---|---|---|---|
|  | 2022 | 2023 | 2024 | 2022 | 2023 | 2024 |
| Developing Asia | 4.2 | 4.8 | 4.8 | 4.4 | 4.2 | 3.3 |
| Caucasus and Central Asia | 5.1 | 4.4 | 4.6 | 12.9 | 10.3 | 7.5 |
| East Asia | 2.8 | 4.6 | 4.2 | 2.3 | 2.3 | 2.0 |
| South Asia | 6.4 | 5.5 | 6.1 | 8.2 | 8.1 | 5.8 |
| Southeast Asia | 5.6 | 4.7 | 5.0 | 5.0 | 4.4 | 3.3 |
| The Pacific | 5.2 | 3.3 | 2.8 | 5.7 | 5.0 | 4.4 |

GDP = gross domestic product.
Source: *Asian Development Outlook* database (accessed 18 May 2023).

---

[a] This box was written by Irfan Qureshi (economist) and David de Padua (economics officer) in the Economic Research and Regional Cooperation Department of the Asian Development Bank.

tightening in advanced economies will significantly shape financial conditions globally and within the region. Monetary policy transmission may also be affected by the degree of market corporate power (**Box 2**). Various headwinds to the regional economic outlook also contribute to ongoing risks to financial conditions.

Higher interest rates could challenge both governments and private sector firms, especially those with relatively high debt levels. Higher interest rates increase debt burdens. In the region, a high debt level in the Lao PDR— where public debt is forecast to reach 128.5% of GDP by 2022, with a majority of debt in foreign currency (104.5% of GDP)—has caused debt sustainability concerns. In May, the International Monetary Fund noted that the debt level in the Lao PDR is expected to remain high as the fiscal consolidation may be insufficient to

pare down debt. Meanwhile, the Lao PDR's debt burden was exacerbated by the depreciation of the kip.

Moreover, higher interest rates reduce asset values and quality. Deteriorating asset quality and valuations have triggered liquidity concerns in advanced economies, which may also pose financial risks in the region. For example, rising private debt in Cambodia and stress in the corporate bond market in Viet Nam may make these economies more prone to such risks. Close monitoring and timely intervention can help support financial stability.

In the medium to longer term, climate-related risks will increasingly be a factor in monetary policy, given that both physical and transition risks can contribute to uncertainty in growth, inflation, and financial stability. This calls for more development of sustainable finance markets (**Box 3**).

## Box 2: Monetary Policy Transmission in an Era of Rising Corporate Market Power— What Can 3,000 Asian Firms Tell Us?

Corporate market power has increased in Asia during the past decade, which can compromise the effectiveness of monetary policy.[a] Although the trajectory of corporate mark-up levels in Asia over this period has been somewhat more muted than the global average, it has risen sharply (De Loecker and Eeckhout 2018). Market power has been a long-standing concern for many policymakers and academic researchers, as it greatly matters for economic welfare and resource allocation (e.g., De Loecker, Eeckhout, and Unger 2020).

A new paper from the Asian Development Bank Institute delves further into this issue by using firm-level data over the period 2013–2021 for more than 3,000 firms across 11 economies in Asia: Hong Kong, China; India; Indonesia; Japan; Malaysia; the People's Republic of China; the Philippines; the Republic of Korea; Singapore; Taipei,China; and Viet Nam. Renzhi and Beirne (2023) find strong empirical support that high corporate market power, as measured by the distribution of firms' mark-ups in the top quartile, weakens the effectiveness of monetary policy transmission.

Firm mark-ups in Asia have increased since 2013, driven by advances in technology-based production and sectoral productivity. In an environment where firms face fewer competitive pressures in the setting of prices, the results

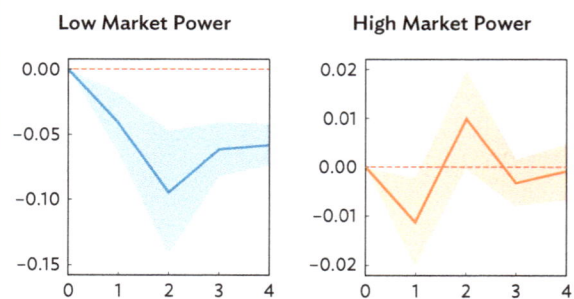

**Figure B2: Impulse Responses of Real Sales to Monetary Policy Shocks—Low vs. High Market Power Firms**

Notes: The figure plots the impulse responses of real sales to a 1 percentage point contractionary monetary policy shock at an annual frequency. Confidence bands (95%) are reported in shaded areas. The vertical axis unit is percentage points, and the horizontal axis refers to the number of years.
Source: Renzhi and Beirne (2023).

indicate that these financial frictions are compounded by an impairment in the monetary policy transmission mechanism. A tightening of monetary policy has the expected dampening effect on firms' real sales for those that have low market power—that is, firms that are in competitive markets with elastic demand for their products and services. For these firms, higher interest rates dampen real sales, thereby enabling

---

[a] This box was written by John Beirne (vice-chair of research and senior research fellow) of the Asian Development Bank Institute in Tokyo and Nuobu Renzhi (assistant professor) at the School of Economics of Capital University of Economics and Business in Beijing.

*continued on next page*

**Box 2** *continued*

the central bank to affect the business cycle. Specifically, a 1 percentage point rise in interest rates leads to a drop in real sales of around 0.09 percentage points after 2 years, with the negative effect dampening somewhat thereafter but exhibiting persistence and statistical significance over the time horizon. For firms with high market power, however, the effect of monetary policy is significant only for the first year and at a magnitude much lower than for firms with low market power (by a factor of around 5). Moreover, the response to the monetary policy shock becomes insignificant after the first year (**Figure B2**).

It is evident, therefore, that where market power is high the monetary policy transmission mechanism is disrupted. The results are robust to several robustness tests, including alternative monetary policy measures, alternative mark-up definitions, and concerns about additional factors that may affect the estimates. Renzhi and Beirne (2023) also find no material difference in the result for emerging versus advanced economies in Asia. In the case of the former, however, the elasticity of real sales is more pronounced and more persistent. This could be related to a higher natural rate of interest in emerging compared to advanced economies and a greater scope for countercyclical monetary policy. Additionally, heterogeneity in the degree of economic freedom, sectoral composition, and financial leverage does not eliminate the heterogeneous effects of monetary policy concerning firms' market power.

**Policy Implications for Central Bankers and Financial Supervisors**

Policymakers in central banks need to be aware that rising market power has made monetary policies less effective, as dominant firms have fewer incentives to adjust their output when the cost of inputs changes. They are also more immune

to shifts in external financing conditions. Excessive growth in corporate market power could lead to higher inflation during economic downturns, with high-markup firms turning negative shocks into higher prices, thereby further impairing effective monetary policy transmission.

Maximizing the effective implementation of monetary policy requires a more level playing field with regard to competition. Policymakers and competition authorities should closely monitor financial stability risks and negative economic repercussions related to the abuse of a dominant position through merger control. Competition policy should be aimed at fostering an efficient market mechanism across all sectors of the economy and competitive price-setting behavior by firms. This helps to compress heterogeneity in market power dynamics and, therefore, enhances the effectiveness of monetary policy transmission. Policies also need to be balanced to continue to encourage innovation and productivity, underscoring the importance of policy coordination across fiscal, industrial, and competition policies.

**References**

De Loecker, Jan, and Jan Eeckhout. 2018. "Global Market Power." National Bureau of Economic Research Working Paper.

De Loecker, Jan, Jan Eeckhout, and Gabriel Unger. 2020. "The Rise of Market Power and the Macroeconomic Implications." *The Quarterly Journal of Economics* 135 (2): 561–644.

Renzhi, Nuobu, and John Beirne. 2023. "Corporate Market Power and Monetary Policy Transmission in Asia." Asian Development Bank Institute Working Paper No. 1635.

# Box 3: Developing Sustainable Finance Markets Requires Proactive Climate Actions from Central Banks

It is becoming increasingly clear that climate risks will exert a major impact on inflation, economic growth, and financial systems.[a] Meanwhile, the global financial system is facing the problem of mispricing due to the presence of low carbon prices that do not adequately reflect the social cost of emitting greenhouse gases. To accelerate the attainment of carbon neutrality, financial institutions need to improve their understanding of climate risks and related risk management. This is essential to foster a sustainable finance market since realizing a carbon-neutral economy requires a large amount of investment and the mobilization of funds for that purpose. If these issues are left unaddressed, the transition process will remain too slow to achieve carbon neutrality. Moreover, climate risks may destabilize financial systems as climate-related physical, transition, and liability risks materialize over time.

Central banks and financial regulators have realized that they can no longer take neutral positions and ignore climate change and other environmental issues. There are several climate-related actions that central banks and financial regulators can take, while climate and other environmental factors can be incorporated into financial stability frameworks, macro climate modeling, and monetary policy operations.

### Coping with Climate-Related Financial Risks to Maintain Financial Stability

Among authorities' possible actions, there is a growing global consensus that central banks and financial regulators should view climate risks as a major financial risk. The Financial Stability Board's roadmap on this subject stressed the need to improve companies' and financial institutions' disclosure and data collection, push financial institutions to perform climate scenario analysis, and encourage financial authorities to improve their surveillance (Financial Stability Board 2021). An increasing number of financial authorities have started to incorporate climate risks into financial stability frameworks as part of their prudential policies. In particular, encouraging banks and other financial institutions to conduct climate scenario analysis and/or stress tests, which has implications for capital adequacy levels, is central to deepening financial institutions' understanding of climate risks and improving their risk management.

The Network of Central Banks and Supervisors on Greening the Financial System, which comprises more than 100 central banks and financial supervisors, provides reference climate scenarios that can be used by financial authorities when performing bottom-up exercises for financial institutions in their jurisdictions. There are possible climate scenarios: (i, ii) orderly (net zero [1.5°C] and below 2°C); (iii, iv) disorderly (delayed 2°C and divergent net zero); and (v, vi) hothouse world (nationally determined contributions scenario and current policies). Compared to the hothouse world scenarios, transition risks are somewhat higher but physical risks are much lower under the orderly scenarios (**Figure B3**). Among them, the three main scenarios are net zero, delayed 2°C, and current policies. More than 30 jurisdictions are implementing climate-scenario analysis. Financial authorities use these scenarios as a baseline and make adjustments by adding country- or region-specific factors. Such analysis can enable financial regulators to examine the potential impact on financial institutions under various climate scenarios. Financial regulators could also use these exercises to promote financial institutions' awareness about potential deficiencies in their climate risk management frameworks, thereby requiring them to improve their risk management practices.

Beyond climate scenario analysis, discussions have emerged in recent years, mainly in Europe, on how to include

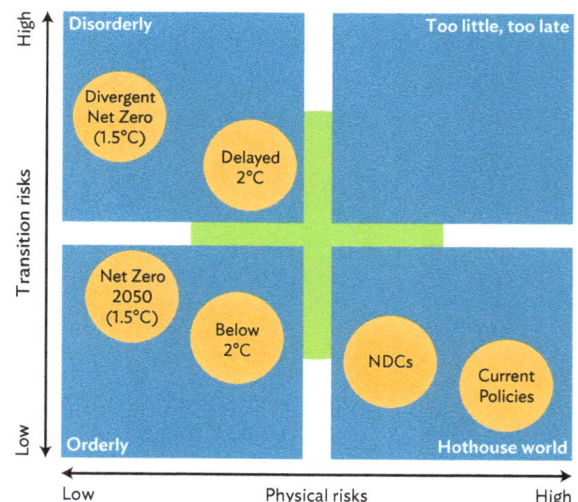

**Figure B3: NGFS' Six Types of Climate Scenarios**

NDC = nationally defined contribution, NGFS = Network of Central Banks and Supervisors on Greening the Financial System.
Source: NGFS (2022).

---

[a] This box was written by Sayuri Shirai, a visiting fellow and advisor for sustainable policies at the Asian Development Bank Institute, a professor at the Faculty of Policy Management of Keio University, and a former policy board member of the Bank of Japan.

*continued on next page*

**Box 3**   *continued*

climate-related financial risks in the capital adequacy requirements applied to banks under the Basel framework—particularly, the standard Pillar 1 and Pillar 2 capital requirements. Rigorous investigations have been undertaken by the Bank of England, the European Central Bank, various European Union financial regulators, the Basel Committee on Banking Supervision, and the Bank for International Settlements (Shirai 2023a). As it takes time to collect reliable, consistent data from financial institutions (and from their corporate counterparties) and to refine methodological approaches, the adoption of the Pillar 1 framework may not be feasible in the near future. Adjusting the standard Pillar 1 instruments for the sake of incorporating climate risks could be challenging since credit risks, for example, are calibrated for a 1-year time horizon based on historical loss data that are not available for climate risks. More forward-looking approaches are necessary when calibrating capital requirements related to climate risks that tend to materialize nonlinearly over time. Thus, the Pillar 2 approach could be more feasible as capital assessments can be made using climate scenario analysis and stress tests more flexibly. Meanwhile, some central banks, such as the People's Bank of China, have already conducted climate stress tests that consider the implications for capital adequacy ratios.

**Central Banks' Monetary Policy Responses to Climate Risks**

There are several possible monetary policy options for central banks to take in contributing to greening the financial market and achieving carbon neutrality goals (Network of Central Banks and Supervisors on Greening the Financial System 2022). **Table B3** shows that these options include asset purchases, credit operations, and collateral utilized in central banks' lending operations for financial institutions.

Asset purchases could take a tilting approach (i.e., increasing the weight of greener assets in total assets purchased) and in some cases a negative screening approach (i.e., divesting assets in case the bond issuer fails to meet climate criteria). Currently, the European Central Bank is the only central bank that incorporates climate criteria into the reinvestment corporate bond framework through a tilting approach, which it has done since October 2022. The reinvestment framework has been used since the net purchasing of financial assets was terminated in early July 2022. Meanwhile, the Bank of England was the first central bank that adopted a tilting approach in its reinvestment corporate bond framework by setting an emissions reduction target on its holdings of corporate bonds—before the decision to sell all the holdings

**Table B3: Green Monetary Policy Actions for Central Banks**

| | |
|---|---|
| **Asset Purchases** | |
| (1) Tilting purchases | Skew asset purchases according to climate-related risks and/or criteria applied at the issuer or asset level. |
| (2) Negative screening | Exclude some assets or issuers from purchases if they fail to meet climate-related criteria. |
| **Credit Operations** | |
| (3) Adjust pricing to reflect counterparties' climate-related lending | Make the interest rate for central bank lending facilities conditional on the extent to which a counterparty's lending (relative to a relevant benchmark) is contributing to climate change mitigation and/or the extent to which they are decarbonizing their business model. |
| (4) Adjust pricing to reflect the composition of pledged collateral | Charge a lower (or higher) interest rate to counterparties that pledge a higher proportion of low-carbon (or carbon-intensive) assets as collateral or set up a credit facility (potentially at concessional rates) accessible only against low-carbon assets. |
| (5) Adjust counterparties' eligiblity | Make access to (some) lending facilities conditional on a counterparty's disclosure of climate-related information or on its carbon-intensive, low-carbon, and green investment. |
| **Collateral** | |
| (6) Adjust haircuts | Adjust haircuts to better account for climate-related risks. Haircuts could also be calibrated such that they go beyond what might be required from a purely risk mitigation perspective in order to incentivize the market for sustainable assets. |
| (7) Negative screening | Exclude otherwise eligible collateral assets based on their issuer-level, climate-related risk profile for debt securities or on the analysis of the carbon performance of underlying assets for pledged pools of loans or securitized products. This could be done in different ways, including adjusting eligibility requirements, tightening risk tolerance, and introducing tighter or specific mobilization rules. |
| (8) Positive screening | Accept sustainable collateral to incentivize banks to lend or capital markets to fund projects and assets that support environmentally friendly activities (e.g., green bonds or sustainability linked assets). This could be done in different ways, including adjusting eligibility requirements, increasing risk tolerance on a limited scale, and relaxing some mobilization rules. |
| (9) Align collateral pools with a climate-related objective | Require counterparties to pledge collateral such that it complies with a climate-related metric at an aggregate pool level. |

Source: Author's compilation based on NFGS (2021).

*continued on next page*

**Box 3** *continued*

of assets, including corporate bonds, was made. A tilting approach appears desirable if it is important to encourage emissions-intensive sectors and companies to make greater efforts to reduce greenhouse gas emissions.

While many central banks conduct short-term credit operations for financial institutions, only a few central banks provide long-term credit operations (i.e., maturity of 1 year or longer). If credit operations are considered as a green monetary policy tool, providing longer-term finance to financial institutions is desirable. Credit operations could take the form of lowering interest rates, conditional upon such financial institutions having a good climate-related lending performance. Central banks could also lower lending rates for financial institutions whose composition of low-carbon assets accepted as collateral is greater. Providing greater access to central banks' lending facilities conditional on financial institutions' climate-related lending performance can also be a policy tool. In this regard, central banks could launch new long-term credit facilities by providing long-term, low-interest finance based on the volume of green loans extended and/or green bond investments. The central bank of Brazil, the Bank of Japan, and the People's Bank of China have adopted environmental criteria into their lending programs (Shirai 2023a, 2023b).

As for foreign reserves, a number of central banks have already begun to integrate climate and other sustainability criteria into their foreign asset management frameworks. One crucial difference between foreign reserve management and domestic asset management—from the perspective of promoting the sustainable finance market—is that the former supports sustainable foreign markets, including green bond markets, while the latter helps to foster domestic markets. The Monetary Authority of Singapore was one of the first central banks in Asia to adopt emissions targets for its investment portfolio, which mostly comprises foreign reserves. The targets are calculated based on the carbon intensity of its equities and corporate bonds portfolio using greenhouse gas emission data (Scopes 1 and 2 emissions).

**Conclusions**

In general, central banks are responsible for achieving price stability under their monetary policy mandate and financial stability under their prudential policy mandate. Therefore, it may be possible for central banks to consider climate risks within their existing mandates. As shown above, central banks increasingly focus on financial stability and have been exploring how to measure climate-related financial risks and improve surveillance. On the other hand, a consensus has not yet emerged as to whether central banks should incorporate climate risks in their price stability mandates and, thus, in their monetary policy frameworks. Some central banks

appear to place more emphasis on climate-related financial risks and prudential perspectives in supervising financial institutions rather than relating climate risks to price stability and monetary policy (Shirai 2023a). For this reason, there are still only a limited number of central banks that conduct green monetary policy.

As governments are expected to accelerate their climate and energy policies to achieve climate neutrality goals, fostering effective green and sustainable financial markets that support a transition toward carbon neutrality will be increasingly pursued in partnership with financial institutions, companies, and other stakeholders. As such viewpoints become widespread, central banks may find it more comfortable to take proactive monetary policy actions to encourage financial institutions to improve climate-related risk management and help to develop sustainable financial markets. Currently, central banks in Europe are taking the lead with these efforts, reflecting their governments' more active climate policy actions. Nonetheless, some central banks in Asia and other emerging market economies are also becoming more visible in this regard.

**References**

Financial Stability Board (FSB). 2021. *FSB Roadmap for Addressing Climate-Related Financial Risks*. https://www.fsb.org/wp-content/uploads/P070721-2.pdf.

Network of Central Banks and Supervisors for Greening the Financial System (NGFS). 2021. "Adapting Central Bank Operations to a Hotter World: Reviewing Some Options." NGFS Technical Document. https://www.ngfs.net/sites/default/files/media/2021/06/17/ngfs_monetary_policy_operations_final.pdf.

————. 2022. "Climate Scenarios for Central Banks and Supervisors." 6 September. https://www.ngfs.net/en/ngfs-climate-scenarios-central-banks-and-supervisors-september-2022.

Sayuri Shirai. 2023a. "Green Central Banking and Regulation to Foster Sustainable Finance." Asian Development Bank Institute Working Paper No. 1361. https://www.adb.org/publications/green-central-banking-and-regulation-foster-sustainable-finance.

————. 2023b. "Central Bank Initiatives Essential for Developing Effective Sustainable Finance Markets." *Asia Pathways*. Asian Development Bank Institute. 2 March. https://www.asiapathways-adbi.org/2023/03/central-bank-initiatives-essential-for-developing-effective-sustainable-finance-markets/.

# Bond Market Developments in the First Quarter of 2023

## Section 1. Size and Composition

**Emerging East Asian local currency (LCY) bond market reached a size of USD23.8 trillion at the end of March, expanding 9.1% from a year earlier.**[3] The annual growth of the region's LCY bonds outstanding exceeded that of the United States (US) (5.7%) and the European Union 20 (EU-20) (2.9%) (**Figure 1**). In terms of overall size, emerging East Asian LCY bond market surpassed that of the EU-20 in 2020 and reached the equivalent of 66.0% of the US bond market at the end of March 2023.

**Quarterly growth in the region's LCY bond market accelerated on increased issuance of Treasury and other government bonds.** Emerging East Asian LCY bond market growth climbed to 2.2% quarter-on-quarter (q-o-q) in the first quarter (Q1) of 2023 from 1.2% q-o-q in the fourth quarter (Q4) of 2022 (**Figure 2** and **Table 1**). Growth was weaker than the 3.1% q-o-q expansion recorded in Q1 2022. Increased issuance of Treasury and other government bonds was the main driver of emerging East Asian LCY bond market growth in Q1 2023, as many of the region's governments frontloaded debt issuance to finance programs supporting economic recovery. Six out of the nine markets in the region posted faster q-o-q growth in Q1 2023 compared to the previous quarter. Smaller markets such as Viet Nam (5.1%), Indonesia (3.5%), and the Philippines (3.1%) posted the most rapid expansions in the region in Q1 2023.

---

**Figure 1: Local Currency Bonds Outstanding in Emerging East Asia, the EU-20, and the United States**

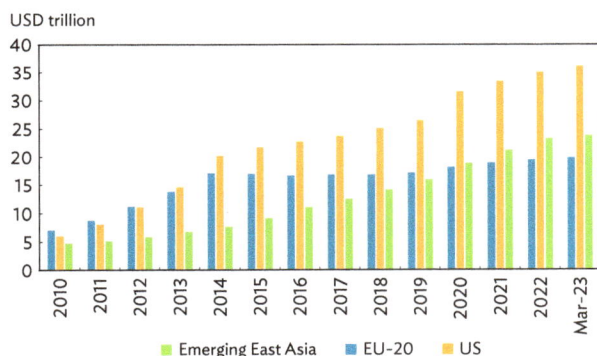

USD trillion

Legend: Emerging East Asia, EU-20, US

EU = European Union, US = United States, USD = United States dollar.

Notes:
1. Emerging East Asia is defined to include the Association of Southeast Asian Nations plus the People's Republic of China; Hong Kong, China; and the Republic of Korea.
2. EU-20 includes EU member markets Austria, Belgium, Croatia, Cyprus, Estonia, Finland, France, Germany, Greece, Ireland, Italy, Latvia, Lithuania, Luxembourg, Malta, the Netherlands, Portugal, Slovakia, Slovenia, and Spain.

Sources: People's Republic of China (CEIC Data Company); Hong Kong, China (Hong Kong Monetary Authority); EU-20 (Bloomberg LP); Indonesia (Bank Indonesia; Directorate General of Budget Financing and Risk Management, Ministry of Finance; and Indonesia Stock Exchange); Republic of Korea (Bank of Korea and KG Zeroin Corporation); Malaysia (Bank Negara Malaysia); Philippines (Bureau of the Treasury and Bloomberg LP); Singapore (Monetary Authority of Singapore and Bloomberg LP); Thailand (Bank of Thailand); United States (Bloomberg LP); and Viet Nam (Vietnam Bond Market Association and Bloomberg LP).

---

**Figure 2: Growth of Select Emerging East Asian Local Currency Bond Markets in the Fourth Quarter of 2022 and the First Quarter of 2023** (q-o-q)

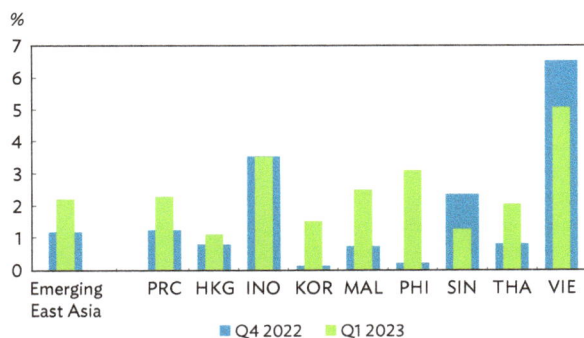

%

Legend: Q4 2022, Q1 2023

HKG = Hong Kong, China; INO = Indonesia; KOR = Republic of Korea; MAL = Malaysia; PHI = Philippines; PRC = People's Republic of China; Q1 = first quarter; Q4 = fourth quarter; q-o-q = quarter-on-quarter; SIN = Singapore; THA = Thailand; VIE = Viet Nam.

Notes:
1. For Singapore, corporate bonds outstanding are based on *AsianBondsOnline* estimates.
2. Growth rates are calculated from local currency base and do not include currency effects. For emerging East Asia, growth figures are based on 31 March 2023 currency exchange rates and do not include currency effects.

Sources: People's Republic of China (CEIC Data Company); Hong Kong, China (Hong Kong Monetary Authority); Indonesia (Bank Indonesia; Directorate General of Budget Financing and Risk Management, Ministry of Finance; and Indonesia Stock Exchange); Republic of Korea (Bank of Korea and KG Zeroin Corporation); Malaysia (Bank Negara Malaysia); Philippines (Bureau of the Treasury and Bloomberg LP); Singapore (Monetary Authority of Singapore and Bloomberg LP); Thailand (Bank of Thailand); and Viet Nam (Vietnam Bond Market Association and Bloomberg LP).

---

[3] Emerging East Asia is defined to include member states of the Association of Southeast Asian Nations (ASEAN) plus the People's Republic of China; Hong Kong, China; and the Republic of Korea.

## Table 1: Size and Composition of Select Emerging East Asian Local Currency Bond Markets

| | Q1 2022 | | Q4 2022 | | Q1 2023 | | | Growth Rate (%) Q1 2023 | |
|---|---|---|---|---|---|---|---|---|---|
| | Amount (USD billion) | % of GDP | Amount (USD billion) | % of GDP | Amount (USD billion) | % share | % of GDP | q-o-q | y-o-y |
| **China, People's Rep. of** | | | | | | | | | |
| Total | 18,755 | 101.5 | 18,463 | 105.2 | 18,957 | 100.0 | 106.5 | 2.3 | 9.6 |
| Treasury and Other Government | 12,049 | 65.2 | 12,122 | 69.1 | 12,489 | 65.9 | 70.2 | 2.7 | 12.4 |
| Central Bank | 2 | 0.01 | 2 | 0.01 | 2 | 0.01 | 0.01 | 0.0 | 0.0 |
| Corporate | 6,704 | 36.3 | 6,338 | 36.1 | 6,465 | 34.1 | 36.3 | 1.6 | 4.6 |
| **Hong Kong, China** | | | | | | | | | |
| Total | 325 | 89.4 | 355 | 98.3 | 357 | 100.0 | 98.3 | 1.1 | 10.0 |
| Treasury and Other Government | 22 | 6.0 | 31 | 8.5 | 29 | 8.1 | 8.0 | (4.9) | 32.4 |
| Government | 152 | 41.8 | 155 | 42.8 | 155 | 43.4 | 42.7 | 0.8 | 2.3 |
| Corporate | 151 | 41.6 | 170 | 47.0 | 173 | 48.5 | 47.7 | 2.6 | 14.6 |
| **Indonesia** | | | | | | | | | |
| Total | 381 | 31.3 | 382 | 30.4 | 411 | 100.0 | 30.6 | 3.5 | 12.5 |
| Treasury and Other Government | 345 | 28.3 | 350 | 27.8 | 377 | 91.8 | 28.1 | 3.8 | 14.0 |
| Central Bank | 5 | 0.4 | 3 | 0.3 | 4 | 0.9 | 0.3 | 3.1 | (17.7) |
| Corporate | 31 | 2.6 | 29 | 2.3 | 30 | 7.3 | 2.2 | 0.5 | (0.5) |
| **Korea, Rep. of** | | | | | | | | | |
| Total | 2,391 | 150.0 | 2,346 | 150.8 | 2,315 | 100.0 | 152.8 | 1.5 | 4.0 |
| Treasury and Other Government | 893 | 56.0 | 907 | 58.3 | 892 | 38.5 | 58.9 | 1.2 | 7.3 |
| Central Bank | 116 | 7.3 | 89 | 5.7 | 94 | 4.1 | 6.2 | 8.4 | (12.9) |
| Corporate | 1,383 | 86.7 | 1,350 | 86.7 | 1,329 | 57.4 | 87.7 | 1.3 | 3.3 |
| **Malaysia** | | | | | | | | | |
| Total | 420 | 125.4 | 424 | 150.8 | 433 | 100.0 | 125.0 | 2.5 | 8.4 |
| Treasury and Other Government | 232 | 69.4 | 238 | 58.3 | 247 | 57.0 | 71.2 | 3.9 | 11.8 |
| Central Bank | 0 | 0.0 | 0.2 | 5.7 | 0.5 | 0.1 | 0.1 | 100.0 | – |
| Corporate | 188 | 56.1 | 185 | 86.7 | 186 | 42.9 | 53.6 | 0.6 | 4.1 |
| **Philippines** | | | | | | | | | |
| Total | 203 | 52.7 | 201 | 50.8 | 212 | 100.0 | 50.9 | 3.1 | 9.8 |
| Treasury and Other Government | 164 | 42.6 | 164 | 41.4 | 173 | 81.6 | 41.5 | 3.4 | 10.8 |
| Central Bank | 8 | 2.1 | 9 | 2.2 | 10 | 4.8 | 2.4 | 15.8 | 35.6 |
| Corporate | 31 | 8.0 | 29 | 7.3 | 29 | 13.6 | 6.9 | (2.2) | (2.0) |
| **Singapore** | | | | | | | | | |
| Total | 447 | 102.2 | 494 | 90.0 | 504 | 100.0 | 104.0 | 1.3 | 10.8 |
| Treasury and Other Government | 164 | 37.5 | 174 | 50.5 | 175 | 34.7 | 36.1 | (0.4) | 4.9 |
| Central Bank | 154 | 35.2 | 186 | 13.8 | 195 | 38.7 | 40.2 | 4.2 | 24.4 |
| Corporate | 129 | 29.6 | 134 | 25.6 | 134 | 26.6 | 27.7 | (0.5) | 2.0 |
| **Thailand** | | | | | | | | | |
| Total | 451 | 91.4 | 452 | 90.0 | 466 | 100.0 | 90.5 | 2.1 | 6.3 |
| Treasury and Other Government | 244 | 49.4 | 253 | 50.5 | 264 | 56.5 | 51.2 | 2.8 | 11.1 |
| Central Bank | 85 | 17.2 | 69 | 13.8 | 68 | 14.6 | 13.2 | (3.0) | (17.4) |
| Corporate | 122 | 24.7 | 129 | 25.6 | 135 | 28.9 | 26.1 | 3.4 | 13.4 |
| **Viet Nam** | | | | | | | | | |
| Total | 95 | 25.1 | 106 | 26.3 | 112 | 100.0 | 27.2 | 5.1 | 21.1 |
| Treasury and Other Government | 67 | 17.6 | 71 | 17.6 | 76 | 67.8 | 18.4 | 6.3 | 17.0 |
| Central Bank | 0.2 | 0.1 | 4 | 1.0 | 5 | 4.2 | 1.1 | 17.3 | 2,423.6 |
| Corporate | 28 | 7.5 | 31 | 7.7 | 31 | 28.0 | 7.6 | 0.7 | 14.2 |
| **Emerging East Asia** | | | | | | | | | |
| Total | 23,469 | 99.1 | 23,222 | 101.7 | 23,768 | 100.0 | 102.4 | 2.2 | 9.1 |
| Treasury and Other Government | 14,180 | 59.9 | 14,311 | 62.7 | 14,723 | 61.9 | 63.5 | 2.6 | 12.0 |
| Central Bank | 521 | 2.2 | 517 | 2.3 | 533 | 2.2 | 2.3 | 3.2 | 4.0 |
| Corporate | 8,768 | 37.0 | 8,394 | 36.7 | 8,512 | 35.8 | 36.7 | 1.6 | 4.6 |
| **Japan** | | | | | | | | | |
| Total | 10,843 | 239.6 | 10,154 | 239.2 | 10,174 | 100.0 | 240.9 | 1.5 | 2.4 |
| Treasury and Other Government | 10,026 | 221.6 | 9,372 | 220.8 | 9,399 | 92.4 | 222.5 | 1.6 | 2.3 |
| Central Bank | 41 | 0.9 | 34 | 0.8 | 33 | 0.3 | 0.8 | (1.7) | (12.2) |
| Corporate | 776 | 17.1 | 748 | 17.6 | 742 | 7.3 | 17.6 | 0.5 | 4.4 |

( ) = negative, – = not applicable, GDP = gross domestic product, q-o-q = quarter-on-quarter, Q1 = first quarter, Q4 = fourth quarter, USD = United States dollar, y-o-y = year-on-year.

Notes:
1. For Singapore, corporate bonds outstanding are based on *AsianBondsOnline* estimates.
2. Corporate bonds include issues by financial institutions.
3. Data for GDP is from CEIC Data Company.
4. Bloomberg LP end-of-period local currency–USD rates are used.
5. Growth rates are calculated from local currency base and do not include currency effects. For emerging East Asia, growth figures are based on 31 March 2023 currency exchange rates and do not include currency effects.

Sources: People's Republic of China (CEIC Data Company); Hong Kong, China (Hong Kong Monetary Authority); Indonesia (Bank Indonesia; Directorate General of Budget Financing and Risk Management, Ministry of Finance; and Indonesia Stock Exchange); Republic of Korea (Bank of Korea and KG Zeroin Corporation); Malaysia (Bank Negara Malaysia); Philippines (Bureau of the Treasury and Bloomberg LP); Singapore (Monetary Authority of Singapore and Bloomberg LP); Thailand (Bank of Thailand); and Viet Nam (Vietnam Bond Market Association and Bloomberg LP).

**LCY bonds outstanding among members of the Association of Southeast Asian Nations (ASEAN) totaled USD2.1 trillion at the end of March, comprising 9.0% of emerging East Asian LCY bond market.** At the end of March, ASEAN's LCY bond market was equivalent to 60.8% of its gross domestic product (GDP). Meanwhile, the People's Republic of China's (PRC) LCY bond market, with outstanding bonds of USD19.0 trillion (106.5% of GDP), accounted for 79.8% of total emerging East Asian LCY bonds outstanding. The Republic of Korea's USD2.3 trillion LCY bond market (152.8% of GDP) was the second largest in the region, accounting for 9.7% of the emerging East Asian LCY bond total. The region's bond market is dominated by Treasury and other government bonds (**Figure 3**). Outstanding Treasury and other government bonds totaled USD14.7 trillion at the end of March, accounting for 61.9% of the region's total bond stock. Six out of the region's nine markets had over half of their outstanding LCY bonds concentrated in Treasury and other government bonds. Corporate bonds comprised 35.8% of the region's LCY bond market at the end of March, while central bank bonds had a minimal 2.2% share.

**A majority of emerging East Asian LCY Treasury bonds are concentrated in medium- to long-term tenors.** Treasury bonds with maturities longer than 5 years accounted for 53.4% of the region's total outstanding Treasury bonds at the end of March (**Figure 4**). The size-weighted tenor of outstanding Treasury bonds in the region was 9.0 years. All markets except for the PRC

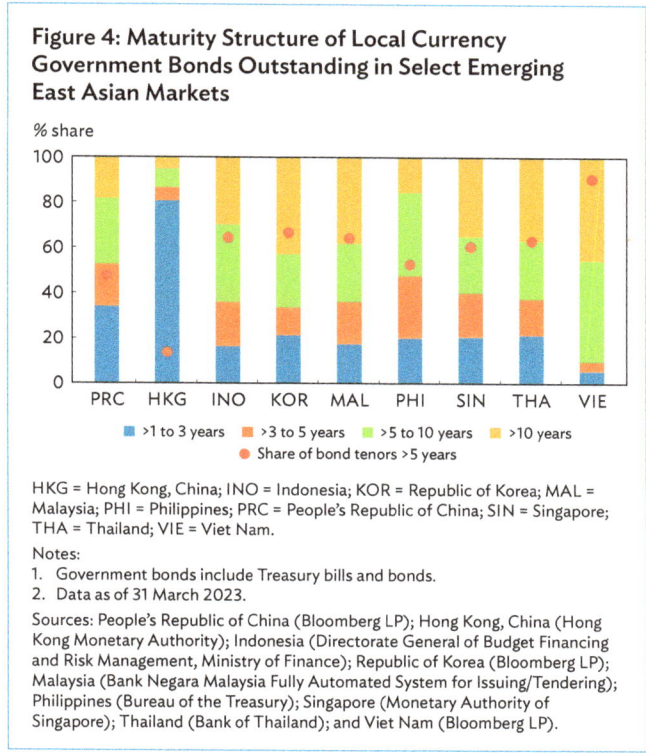

Figure 4: Maturity Structure of Local Currency Government Bonds Outstanding in Select Emerging East Asian Markets

HKG = Hong Kong, China; INO = Indonesia; KOR = Republic of Korea; MAL = Malaysia; PHI = Philippines; PRC = People's Republic of China; SIN = Singapore; THA = Thailand; VIE = Viet Nam.

Notes:
1. Government bonds include Treasury bills and bonds.
2. Data as of 31 March 2023.

Sources: People's Republic of China (Bloomberg LP); Hong Kong, China (Hong Kong Monetary Authority); Indonesia (Directorate General of Budget Financing and Risk Management, Ministry of Finance); Republic of Korea (Bloomberg LP); Malaysia (Bank Negara Malaysia Fully Automated System for Issuing/Tendering); Philippines (Bureau of the Treasury); Singapore (Monetary Authority of Singapore); Thailand (Bank of Thailand); and Viet Nam (Bloomberg LP).

and Hong Kong, China had over half of their Treasury bonds with maturities longer than 5 years. Treasuries with maturities of 3 years or less accounted for 33.9% of total Treasury bonds in the PRC and 80.4% in Hong Kong, China.

**Banks and insurance and pension funds remained the two largest investor groups in most LCY government bond markets in the region at the end of March (Figure 5).** Aside from these two investor groups, the central bank also holds almost one-fifth of LCY government bonds outstanding in Indonesia. Bank Indonesia started purchasing government bonds as part of its pandemic response in 2020. The central bank continues to support the bond market as part of its macroprudential policy mix by buying and selling government bonds in the secondary market. In the PRC, banks held over two-thirds of LCY government bonds outstanding at the end of March. In the Philippines, banks and other groups—including individuals, government institutions, and custodians—are the two largest investor groups in the LCY bond market. The investor profiles of LCY government bond markets in the Republic of Korea, Malaysia, and Thailand have generally become more diverse over the past several quarters, as evidenced by declining Herfindahl–Hirschman Index scores, while in

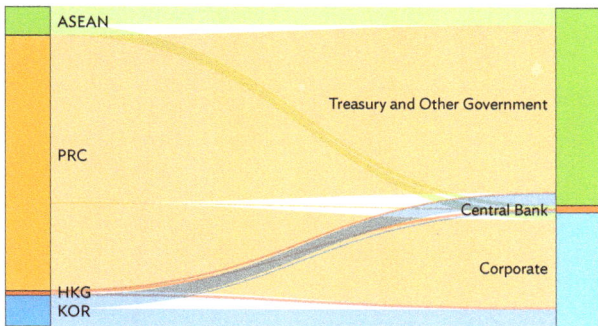

Figure 3: Local Currency Bonds Outstanding by Economy and Type of Bond at the end of March 2023

ASEAN = Association of Southeast Asian Nations; HKG = Hong Kong, China; KOR = Republic of Korea; PRC = People's Republic of China.

Note: ASEAN comprises the markets of Indonesia, Malaysia, the Philippines, Singapore, Thailand, and Viet Nam.

Source: *AsianBondsOnline* calculations based on various local sources.

**Figure 5: Investor Profiles of Local Currency Government Bonds in Select Emerging East Asian Markets**

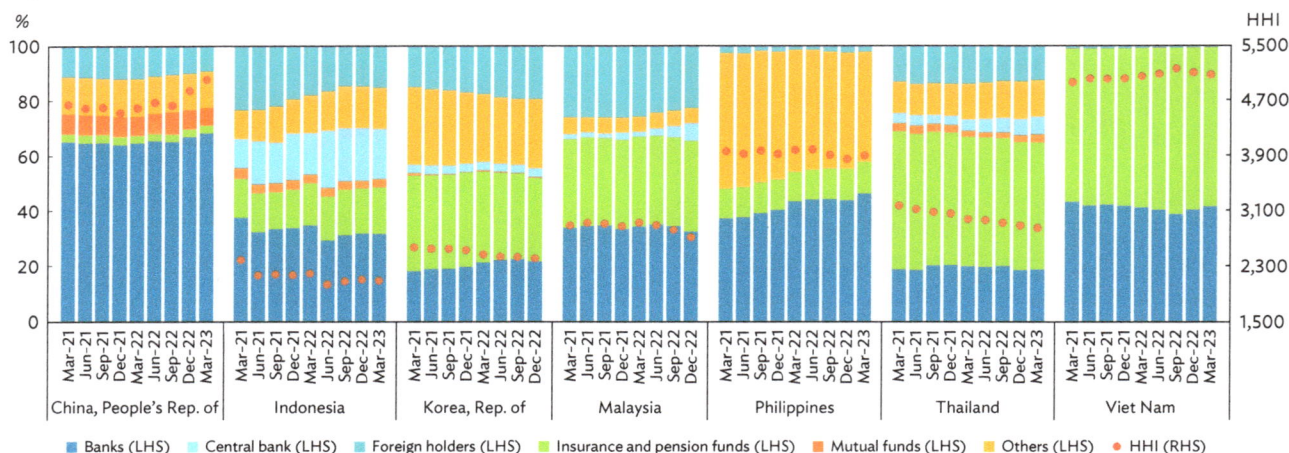

LHS = left-hand side, HHI = Herfindahl–Hirschman Index, RHS = right-hand side.
Notes:
1. Data for the Republic of Korea and Malaysia are up to December 2022.
2. "Others" include government institutions, individuals, securities companies, custodians, private corporations, and all other investors not elsewhere classified.
3. The Herfindahl–Hirschman Index is a commonly accepted measure of market concentration. In this case, the index was used to measure the investor profile diversification of the local currency bond markets and is calculated by summing the squared share of each investor group in the bond market.

Sources: People's Republic of China (CEIC Data Company); Indonesia (Directorate General of Budget Financing and Risk Management, Ministry of Finance); Republic of Korea (Bank of Korea); Malaysia (Bank Negara Malaysia); Philippines (Bureau of the Treasury); Thailand (Bank of Thailand); and Viet Nam (Ministry of Finance).

Viet Nam, only two groups—banks and insurance and pensions funds—are essentially the major investors (**Figure 5**). Foreign holdings of most LCY government bonds in the region have been on a downward trend since Q2 2022, as foreign inflows weakened amid monetary tightening by the US Federal Reserve.

## Section 2. Local Currency Bond Issuance

**LCY bond issuance in emerging East Asia tallied USD2.3 trillion in Q1 2023, with most emerging East Asian markets seeing q-o-q increases in LCY bond issuance.** Overall growth in LCY bond issuance in the region rebounded strongly in Q1 2023, rising 6.2% q-o-q and 12.1% y-o-y after posting contractions of 6.1% q-o-q and 1.2% y-o-y in Q4 2022. The aggregate issuance of emerging East Asian economies in Q1 2023 was equivalent to 55.8% of total issuance in the US (USD4.2 trillion) during the same period, while it exceeded the EU-20's aggregate issuance (USD1.1 trillion) by over twofold. ASEAN markets posted growth of 7.6% q-o-q in Q1 2023 following a contraction of 6.3% q-o-q in Q4 2022. ASEAN's share of regional LCY bond issuance inched up to 21.9% during the quarter from 21.6% in Q4 2022 (**Figure 6**). The PRC and the Republic of Korea, the most active issuers of LCY bonds in the region, recorded marginal declines in their shares of

**Figure 6: Local Currency Bond Issuance in Select Emerging East Asian Markets**

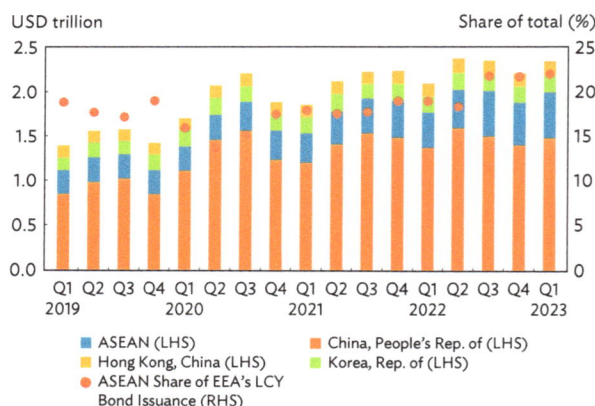

ASEAN = Association of Southeast Asian Nations, EEA = emerging East Asia, LCY = local currency, LHS = left-hand side, Q1 = first quarter, Q2 = second quarter, Q3 = third quarter, Q4 = fourth quarter, RHS = right-hand side, USD = United States dollar.
Notes:
1. ASEAN comprises the markets of Indonesia, Malaysia, the Philippines, Singapore, Thailand, and Viet Nam.
2. Figures were computed based on 31 March 2023 currency exchange rates and do not include currency effects.

Sources: People's Republic of China (CEIC Data Company); Hong Kong, China (Hong Kong Monetary Authority); Indonesia (Bank Indonesia; Directorate General of Budget Financing and Risk Management, Ministry of Finance; and Indonesia Stock Exchange); Republic of Korea (Bank of Korea and KG Zeroin Corportation); Malaysia (Bank Negara Malaysia); Philippines (Bureau of the Treasury and Bloomberg LP); Singapore (Monetary Authority of Singapore and Bloomberg LP); Thailand (Bank of Thailand); and Viet Nam (Vietnam Bond Market Association and Bloomberg LP).

the regional issuance total in Q1 2023 from the previous quarter—from 63.4% to 63.1% and from 8.2% to 8.1%, respectively. In the PRC, issuance climbed 5.7% q-o-q in Q1 2023, reversing the 6.7% q-o-q decline posted in Q4 2022. In the same period, the Republic of Korea's issuance growth accelerated to 4.7% q-o-q from 0.3% q-o-q in the previous quarter. Hong Kong, China posted the region's largest q-o-q increase in Q1 2023 at 7.8%.

**Treasury and other government bond issuance reached USD1.0 trillion and accounted for 43.0% of emerging East Asian LCY bond issuance in Q1 2023, up from a 40.7% share in Q4 2022 (Figure 7).** The PRC dominated emerging East Asia's issuance of Treasury and other government bonds (USD859.7 billion) in Q1 2023, accounting for 85.5% of the regional public issuance total, slightly lower than its 86.7% share in Q4 2022. ASEAN economies posted strong growth in Treasury and other government bond issuance (USD101.6 billion) of 20.8% q-o-q in Q1 2023, reversing a contraction of 18.6% in Q4 2022, due to frontloading issuance policies in some markets. Issuance in the Philippines ramped up in Q1 2023, driven by Retail Treasury Bond issuance of PHP283.7 billion in February. Similarly, Indonesia raised IDR22.2 trillion from the sale of nontradable Savings Bond Ritel in January. The Republic of Korea's issuance of Treasury and other government bonds (USD43.8 billion) increased 27.2% q-o-q in Q1 2023, following a decline of

25.9% q-o-q in Q4 2022, as it aimed to frontload about 65% of its budget spending in the first half of the year. Meanwhile, central bank bond issuance accounted for 22.7% of the region's total LCY bond issuance. ASEAN economies are active issuers of central bank bonds, accounting for 71.8% of total regional central bank bond issuance during the quarter.

**The region's corporate bond issuance moderated amid rising interest rates.** Emerging East Asia corporate bond issuance reached USD799.5 billion in Q1 2023, down from USD809.1 billion (based on current rates) in Q4 2022, comprising 34.2% of the region's total LCY bond issuance in Q1 2023 (**Table 2**). The regional contraction in the issuance of corporate bonds was driven by elevated borrowing costs and heightened uncertainties over the monetary direction of the Federal Reserve and fears of contagion arising from banking sector turmoil in the US and Europe. The PRC led the issuance of corporate bonds with a 76.9% share of the regional total, while the Republic of Korea accounted for a 15.1% share. ASEAN markets comprised only 3.6% of regional LCY corporate bond issuance, reflecting the need for policy initiatives to further the development of corporate bond markets.

**Regional Treasury issuance in Q1 2023 was concentrated in medium- to long-term financing.** Of all Treasury bonds issued during the quarter, 57.7% carried maturities of over 5 years (**Figure 8**). Nearly all emerging East Asian markets in Q1 2023 issued more than 50% of bonds with maturities beyond 5 years, with Hong Kong, China (38.5%) as the exception. Treasury bonds issued in emerging East Asia had a size-weighted average maturity of 6.9 years in Q1 2023, up from 5.9 years in the prior quarter.

## Section 3. Intra-Regional Bond Issuance

**Emerging East Asian intra-regional bond issuance declined on lower issuance from the Republic of Korea.** The region's issuances of intra-regioal bonds moderated to USD11.6 billion in Q1 2023 from USD12.1 billion in Q4 2022, posting a 3.8% q-o-q decline (**Figure 9**).[4] The decline in the intra-regional issuance volume was driven by the Republic of Korea, whose bond issuance decreased 90.0% q-o-q in Q1 2023, offsetting the increases in issuance in Hong Kong, China and Malaysia, as well as new issuances from the

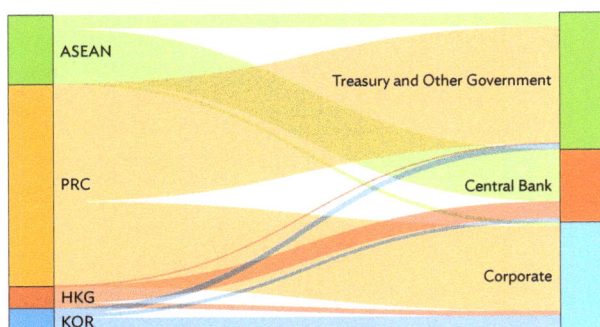

**Figure 7: Local Currency Bond Issuance in the First Quarter of 2023 by Economy and Type of Bond**

ASEAN = Association of Southeast Asian Nations; HKG = Hong Kong, China; KOR = Republic of Korea; PRC = People's Republic of China.

Note: ASEAN comprises the markets of Indonesia, Malaysia, the Philippines, Singapore, Thailand, and Viet Nam.

Source: *AsianBondsOnline* calculations based on various local sources.

---

[4] Intra-regional bond issuance is defined as emerging East Asian bond issuance denominated in a member's currency excluding the issuer's home currency.

**Table 2: Local Currency-Denominated Bond Issuance** (gross)

| | Q1 2022 | | Q4 2022 | | Q1 2023 | | Growth Rate (%) Q1 2023 | |
|---|---|---|---|---|---|---|---|---|
| | Amount (USD billion) | % share | Amount (USD billion) | % share | Amount (USD billion) | % share | q-o-q | y-o-y |
| **China, People's Rep. of** | | | | | | | | |
| Total | 1,481 | 100.0 | 1,390 | 100.0 | 1,475 | 100.0 | 5.7 | 8.0 |
| Treasury and Other Government | 747 | 50.4 | 773 | 55.6 | 860 | 58.3 | 10.8 | 24.8 |
| Central Bank | 0 | 0.0 | 0 | 0.0 | 0 | 0.0 | – | – |
| Corporate | 734 | 49.6 | 616 | 44.4 | 615 | 41.7 | (0.6) | (9.1) |
| **Hong Kong, China** | | | | | | | | |
| Total | 148 | 100.0 | 150 | 100.0 | 161 | 100.0 | 7.8 | 9.0 |
| Treasury and Other Government | 0.4 | 0.3 | 0.8 | 0.5 | 1 | 0.6 | 30.0 | 136.4 |
| Government | 120 | 81.0 | 124 | 82.9 | 124 | 77.3 | 0.6 | 4.0 |
| Corporate | 28 | 18.7 | 25 | 16.6 | 35 | 22.0 | 43.3 | 28.7 |
| **Indonesia** | | | | | | | | |
| Total | 46 | 100.0 | 39 | 100.0 | 36 | 100.0 | (10.0) | (17.3) |
| Treasury and Other Government | 17 | 36.4 | 15 | 39.7 | 16 | 45.1 | 2.2 | 2.4 |
| Central Bank | 26 | 57.7 | 22 | 55.8 | 18 | 49.8 | (19.6) | (28.5) |
| Corporate | 3 | 5.9 | 2 | 4.5 | 2 | 5.0 | 1.8 | (29.1) |
| **Korea, Rep. of** | | | | | | | | |
| Total | 193 | 100.0 | 187 | 100.0 | 190 | 100.0 | 4.7 | 5.8 |
| Treasury and Other Government | 56 | 29.1 | 35 | 19.0 | 44 | 23.0 | 27.2 | (16.2) |
| Central Bank | 25 | 12.9 | 19 | 10.3 | 26 | 13.5 | 37.5 | 11.0 |
| Corporate | 112 | 58.0 | 132 | 70.7 | 120 | 63.4 | (6.2) | 15.7 |
| **Malaysia** | | | | | | | | |
| Total | 19 | 100.0 | 27 | 100.0 | 23 | 100.0 | (14.4) | 25.5 |
| Treasury and Other Government | 12 | 61.4 | 10 | 37.7 | 16 | 68.0 | 54.4 | 39.0 |
| Central Bank | 0 | 0.0 | 0.3 | 1.0 | 0.5 | 2.0 | 66.7 | – |
| Corporate | 7 | 38.6 | 17 | 61.3 | 7 | 30.0 | (58.0) | (2.3) |
| **Philippines** | | | | | | | | |
| Total | 47 | 100.0 | 39 | 100.0 | 50 | 100.0 | 24.7 | 10.9 |
| Treasury and Other Government | 18 | 39.4 | 7 | 19.1 | 17 | 34.8 | 127.3 | (1.9) |
| Central Bank | 25 | 54.3 | 29 | 75.0 | 32 | 64.3 | 6.9 | 31.2 |
| Corporate | 3 | 6.3 | 2 | 5.9 | 0.4 | 0.9 | (81.7) | (84.7) |
| **Singapore** | | | | | | | | |
| Total | 215 | 100.0 | 279 | 100.0 | 295 | 100.0 | 5.0 | 35.2 |
| Treasury and Other Government | 25 | 11.8 | 28 | 9.9 | 29 | 9.9 | 5.4 | 13.7 |
| Central Bank | 187 | 87.4 | 250 | 89.4 | 264 | 89.4 | 4.9 | 38.3 |
| Corporate | 2 | 0.8 | 2 | 0.7 | 2 | 0.7 | 7.2 | 16.3 |
| **Thailand** | | | | | | | | |
| Total | 65 | 100.0 | 64 | 100.0 | 68 | 100.0 | 5.1 | 7.8 |
| Treasury and Other Government | 18 | 27.3 | 18 | 28.1 | 18 | 26.3 | (1.7) | 3.6 |
| Central Bank | 34 | 52.3 | 31 | 49.4 | 34 | 50.1 | 6.6 | 3.3 |
| Corporate | 13 | 20.4 | 14 | 22.5 | 16 | 23.6 | 10.2 | 24.8 |
| **Viet Nam** | | | | | | | | |
| Total | 5 | 100.0 | 23 | 100.0 | 40 | 100.0 | 73.0 | 786.2 |
| Treasury and Other Government | 2 | 39.0 | 4 | 19.3 | 5 | 12.9 | 15.9 | 194.2 |
| Central Bank | 1 | 29.9 | 18 | 80.0 | 34 | 84.0 | 81.8 | 2,389.1 |
| Corporate | 1 | 31.1 | 0.2 | 0.7 | 1 | 3.0 | 639.3 | (13.7) |
| **Emerging East Asia** | | | | | | | | |
| Total | 2,217 | 100.0 | 2,197 | 100.0 | 2,337 | 100.0 | 6.2 | 12.1 |
| Treasury and Other Government | 895 | 40.4 | 892 | 40.6 | 1,006 | 43.0 | 12.4 | 21.1 |
| Central Bank | 419 | 18.9 | 494 | 22.5 | 532 | 22.7 | 7.1 | 27.5 |
| Corporate | 903 | 40.7 | 810 | 36.9 | 799 | 34.2 | (1.2) | (4.5) |
| **Japan** | | | | | | | | |
| Total | 463 | 100.0 | 481 | 100.0 | 489 | 100.0 | 3.0 | 15.2 |
| Treasury and Other Government | 444 | 95.9 | 448 | 93.1 | 466 | 95.2 | 5.3 | 14.5 |
| Central Bank | 0 | 0.0 | 0 | 0.0 | 0 | 0.0 | – | – |
| Corporate | 19 | 4.1 | 33 | 6.9 | 23 | 4.8 | (28.5) | 32.5 |

( ) = negative, – = not applicable, Q1 = first quarter, Q4 = fourth quarter, q-o-q = quarter-on-quarter, USD = United States dollar, y-o-y = year-on-year.

Notes:
1.  Corporate bonds include issues by financial institutions.
2.  Bloomberg LP end-of-period local currency–USD rates are used.
3.  Growth rates are calculated from local currency base and do not include currency effects. For emerging East Asia, growth figures are based on 31 March 2023 currency exchange rates and do not include currency effects.

Sources: People's Republic of China (CEIC Data Company); Hong Kong, China (Hong Kong Monetary Authority); Indonesia (Bank Indonesia; Directorate General of Budget Financing and Risk Management, Ministry of Finance; and Indonesia Stock Exchange); Republic of Korea (Bank of Korea and KG Zeroin Corporation); Malaysia (Bank Negara Malaysia); Philippines (Bureau of the Treasury and Bloomberg LP); Singapore (Monetary Authority of Singapore and Bloomberg LP); Thailand (Bank of Thailand); and Viet Nam (Vietnam Bond Market Association and Bloomberg LP); and Japan (Japan Securities Dealers Association).

## Figure 8: Maturity Structure of Local Currency Government Bond Issuance in Emerging East Asia

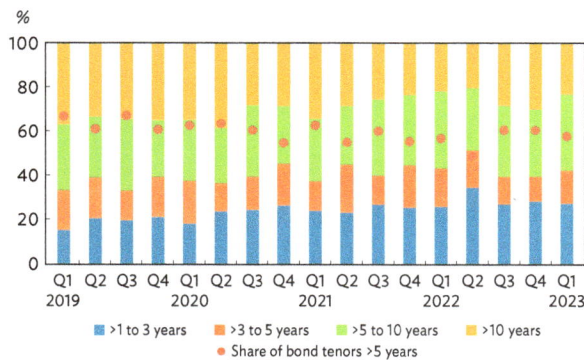

Q1 = first quarter, Q2 = second quarter, Q3 = third quarter, Q4 = fourth quarter.

Note: Figures were computed based on 31 March 2023 currency exchange rates and do not include currency effects.

Source: *AsianBondsOnline* calculations based on various local sources.

## Figure 9: Intra-Regional Bond Issuance in Select Emerging East Asian Economies

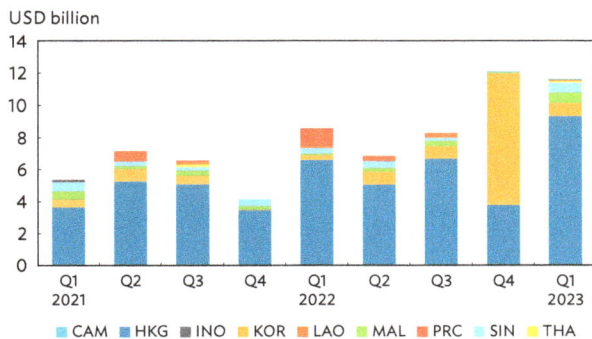

CAM = Cambodia; HKG = Hong Kong, China; INO = Indonesia; KOR = Republic of Korea; LAO = Lao People's Democratic Republic; MAL = Malaysia; PRC = People's Republic of China; Q1 = first quarter; Q2 = second quarter; Q3 = third quarter; Q4 = fourth quarter; SIN = Singapore; THA = Thailand; USD = United States dollar.

Source: *AsianBondsOnline* calculations based on Bloomberg LP data.

## Figure 10: Intra-Regional Bond Issuance in Emerging East Asia by Economy, Currency, and Sector in the First Quarter of 2023

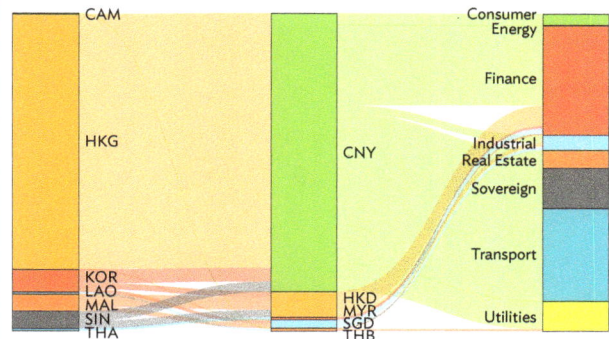

CAM = Cambodia; CNY = Chinese yuan; HKD = Hong Kong dollar; HKG = Hong Kong, China; KOR = Republic of Korea; LAO = Lao People's Democratic Republic; MAL = Malaysia; MYR = Malaysian riggit; SGD = Singapore dollar; SIN = Singapore; THA = Thailand; THB = Thai baht.

Source: *AsianBondsOnline* calculations based on Bloomberg LP data.

Lao People's Democratic Republic, Singapore, and Thailand. Monthly intra-regional issuance volumes amounted to USD5.4 billion, USD3.0 billion, and USD3.3 billion in January, February, and March, respectively. Compared to Q1 2022, total intra-regional bond issuance increased 35.5% y-o-y from USD8.6 billion.

**The Chinese yuan dominated intra-regional bond issuance in Q1 2023, accounting for 87.7% of the emerging East Asian total on issuance of USD10.2 billion (Figure 10).** Institutions from

Hong Kong, China; the Republic of Korea; and Singapore issued intra-regional bonds denominated in Chinese yuan during the quarter. Hong Kong, China was the largest source of intra-regional bonds in Q1 2023 with USD9.4 billion, accounting for 80.5% of the emerging East Asian total.

**The financial sector was the largest source of intra-regional bond issuance in emerging East Asia in Q1 2023, comprising 34.8% of the regional total.** However, the financial sector issuance posted a contraction of 55.6% q-o-q in Q1 2023, with its intra-regional issuance declining to USD4.0 billion from USD9.1 billion in Q4 2022. The transportation and sovereign sectors were the second- and third-largest issuers of intra-regional bonds in Q1 2023, respectively, with regional shares of 29.1% and 12.5%.

## Section 4. G3 Currency Bond Issuance

**Emerging East Asia's issuance of G3 currency bonds reached USD58.4 billion in Q1 2023, the most since Q2 2022 (Figure 11).** On an annual basis, G3 currency bond issuance declined 23.1% from Q1 2022 due to the high-interest-rate environment and various headwinds to the global economic outlook. The region's G3 issuance was largely dragged down by the 55.0% y-o-y decline in issuance from the PRC, the largest G3 currency bond issuer in emerging East Asia. ASEAN markets accounted for 19.6% of the total G3 currency bonds

**Figure 11: Monthly G3 Currency Bond Issuance in Select Emerging East Asian Markets**

USD billion

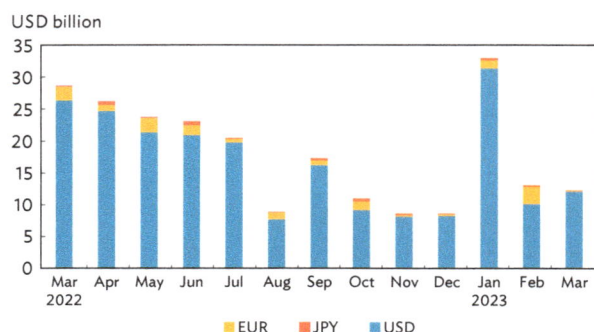

EUR = euro, JPY = Japanese yen, USD = United States dollar.
Notes:
1. Emerging East Asia is defined to include member states of the Association of Southeast Asian Nations (ASEAN) plus the People's Republic of China; Hong Kong, China; and the Republic of Korea.
2. G3 currency bonds are denominated in either euros, Japanese yen, or United States dollars.
3. Figures were computed based on 31 March 2023 currency exchange rates and do not include currency effects.

Source: *AsianBondsOnline* calculations based on Bloomberg LP data.

**Figure 13: Currency Breakdown of G3 Currency Bond Issuance in Emerging East Asia**

Q1 2022 | Q1 2023

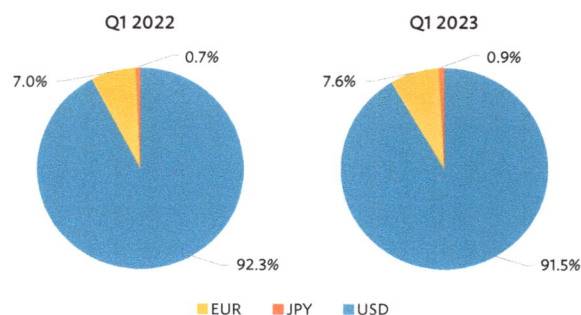

EUR = euro, JPY = Japanese yen, Q1 = first quarter, USD = United States dollar.
Notes:
1. Emerging East Asia is defined to include member states of the Association of Southeast Asian Nations (ASEAN) plus the People's Republic of China; Hong Kong, China; and the Republic of Korea.
2. G3 currency bonds are denominated in either euros, Japanese yen, or United States dollars.
3. Figures were computed based on 31 March 2023 currency exchange rates and do not include currency effects.

Source: *AsianBondsOnline* calculations based on Bloomberg LP data.

**Figure 12: G3 Currency Bond Issuance in Emerging East Asia in the First Quarter of 2023**

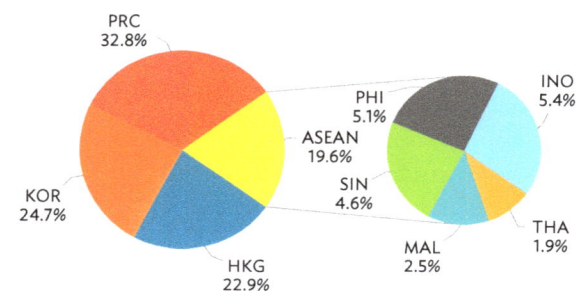

ASEAN = Association of Southeast Asian Nations; HKG = Hong Kong, China; INO = Indonesia; KOR = Republic of Korea; MAL = Malaysia; PHI = Philippines; PRC = People's Republic of China; SIN = Singapore; THA = Thailand.
Note: G3 currency bonds are denominated in either euros, Japanese yen, or United States dollars.
Source: *AsianBondsOnline* calculations based on Bloomberg LP data.

issued in emerging East Asia in Q1 2023 (**Figure 12**), which was higher than their corresponding share of 16.1% in Q1 2022. However, total G3 issuance from ASEAN members contracted 6.2% y-o-y to USD11.5 billion in Q1 2023. Among ASEAN markets, Indonesia and the Philippines led in terms of G3 currency bond issuance with USD3.2 billion and USD3.0 billion, respectively. Cambodia, the Lao People's Democratic Republic, and Viet Nam did not issue any G3 currency bond in Q1 2023. In the same quarter, USD-denominated issuance

accounted for 91.5% of total regional G3 currency bond issuance (**Figure 13**). Bond issuances in US dollars, euros, and Japanese yen all contracted in Q1 2023 from the previous year, with USD-denominated bonds declining the most (23.7% y-o-y) on aggressive US monetary tightening.

## Section 5. Yield Curve Movements

**Between 1 March and 2 June, LCY government bond yield curves shifted downward for most regional markets, particularly at the longer end (Figure 14).** The declines were largely driven by residual inflationary pressure and moderating monetary tightening by regional central banks. Some markets witnessed a downward shift for all tenors. However, in Malaysia, the Philippines, and Thailand, bond yields at the shorter end of the curve rose following central bank interest rate hikes. Viet Nam's yield curve saw the largest downward shift, with an average yield decline of 136 bps, following the State Bank of Vietnam's two consecutive 50 bps rate cuts on the refinancing rate, effective 3 April and 25 May, to spur economic growth.

**Figure 14: Benchmark Yield Curves—Local Currency Government Bonds**

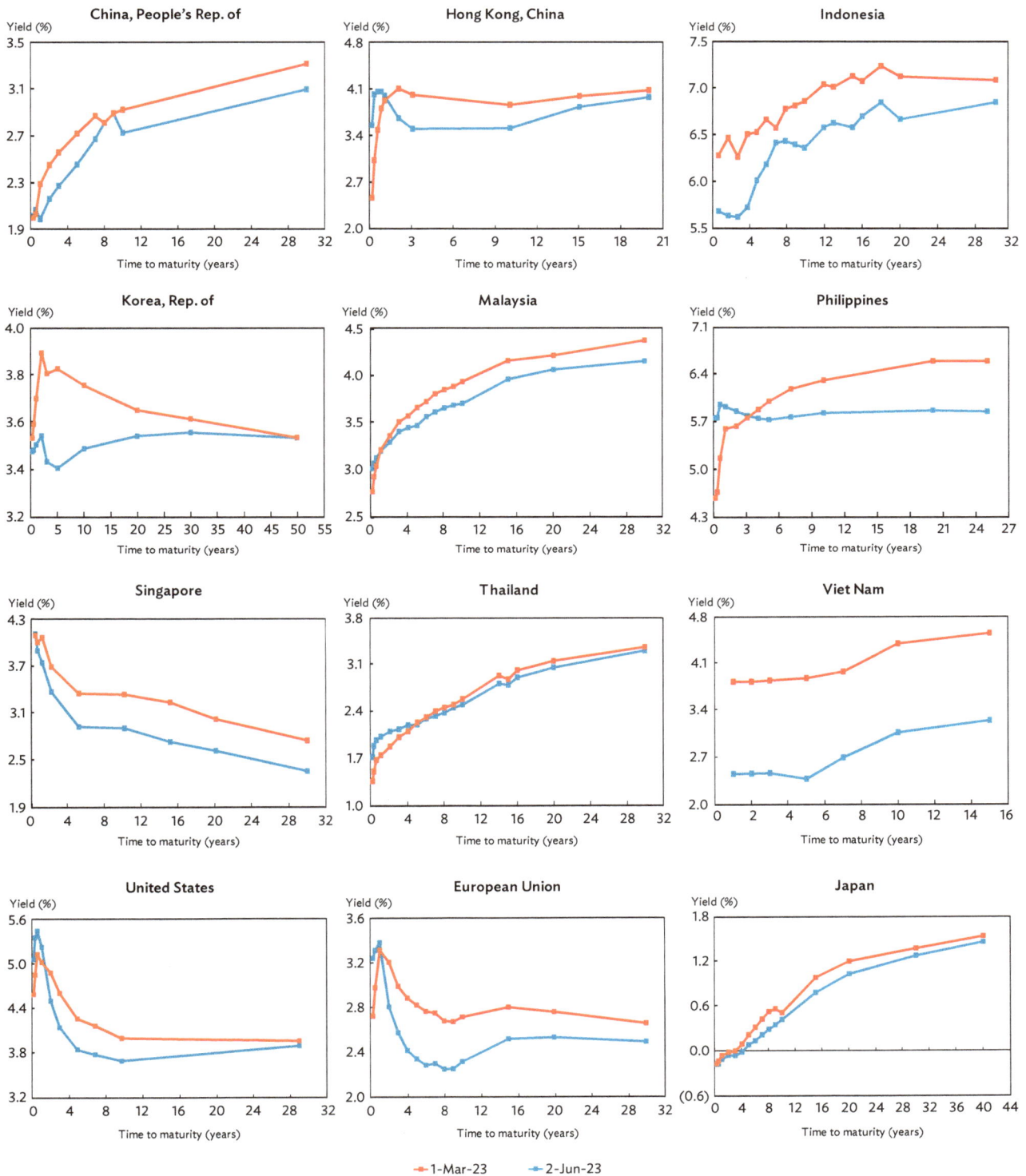

China, People's Rep. of

Hong Kong, China

Indonesia

Korea, Rep. of

Malaysia

Philippines

Singapore

Thailand

Viet Nam

United States

European Union

Japan

—■— 1-Mar-23   —■— 2-Jun-23

( ) = negative.
Sources: Based on data from Bloomberg LP and Thai Bond Market Association.

# Recent Developments in ASEAN+3 Sustainable Bond Markets

Sustainable bond market growth in ASEAN+3 moderated in the first quarter (Q1) of 2023, with bonds outstanding reaching USD633.9 billion at the end of March.[5] Overall growth eased to 5.9% quarter-on-quarter (q-o-q) and 30.7% year-on-year (y-o-y) in Q1 2023, down from 12.4% q-o-q and 38.4% y-o-y in the fourth quarter (Q4) of 2022. Meanwhile, global sustainable bond market growth inched up to 6.2% q-o-q in Q1 2023 from 5.6% q-o-q in Q4 2022, but y-o-y growth slowed to 25.5% from 28.0% over the same period. By the end of March, ASEAN+3 remained the second-largest sustainable bond market in the world with a 17.7% share of the global total, while the European Union 20 (EU-20) had the largest market with a 38.6% share (**Figure 15**).

The ASEAN+3 sustainable bond market needs further development to provide more local currency (LCY) and long-term financing. Despite rapid growth, sustainable bonds comprise a relatively small share of total bond financing in ASEAN+3. ASEAN+3's sustainable bond market comprised 1.8% of the overall ASEAN+3 bond market at the end of March, which was lower than the EU-20 sustainable bond market's corresponding share of 6.6%. By the end of March, green bonds (66.1%), LCY financing (64.0%), and private sector financing (77.1%) comprised most of the ASEAN+3 sustainable bond market (**Figure 16**). In comparison, the EU-20's sustainable bond market had a similar share of green bonds (64.8%) and higher shares of LCY financing (87.9%) and public sector financing (46.1%). In terms of maturity, ASEAN+3 sustainable bonds outstanding had

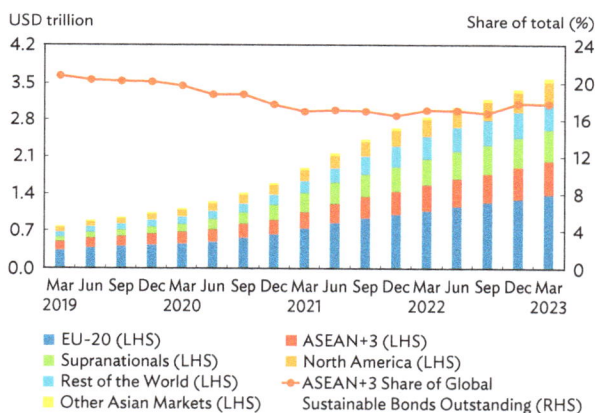

**Figure 15: Global Sustainable Bonds Outstanding**

ASEAN+3 = Association of Southeast Asian Nations plus the People's Republic of China; Hong Kong, China; Japan; and the Republic of Korea; EU = European Union; LHS = left-hand side; RHS = right-hand side; USD = United States dollar.
Notes:
1. EU-20 includes EU member markets Austria, Belgium, Croatia, Cyprus, Estonia, Finland, France, Germany, Greece, Ireland, Italy, Latvia, Lithuania, Luxembourg, Malta, the Netherlands, Portugal, Slovakia, Slovenia, and Spain.
2. Data include both local currency and foreign currency issues.
Source: *AsianBondsOnline* calculations based on Bloomberg LP data.

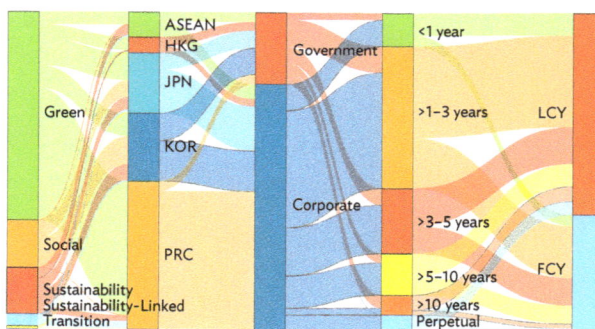

**Figure 16: Market Profile of Outstanding ASEAN+3 Sustainable Bonds at the End of March 2023**

ASEAN = Association of Southeast Asian Nations; FCY = foreign currency; HKG = Hong Kong, China; JPN = Japan; KOR = Republic of Korea; LCY = local currency; PRC = People's Republic of China.
Notes:
1. ASEAN+3 is defined to include member states of the Association of Southeast Asian Nations (ASEAN) plus the People's Republic of China; Hong Kong, China; Japan; and the Republic of Korea.
2. ASEAN comprises the markets of Indonesia, Malaysia, the Philippines, Singapore, Thailand, and Viet Nam.
Source: *AsianBondsOnline* calculations based on Bloomberg LP data.

---

[5] ASEAN+3 is defined to include member states of the Association of Southeast Asian Nations (ASEAN) plus the People's Republic of China; Hong Kong, China; Japan; and the Republic of Korea.

a size-weighted average of 4.4 years at the end of March, half of the EU-20's size-weighted average of 8.8 years. Sustainable bonds with maturities of over 5 years accounted for 24.0% of the ASEAN+3 sustainable bond market, while the corresponding share for the EU-20 was 59.2% (**Figure 17**).

**ASEAN+3's sustainable bond issuance declined in Q1 2023 amid uncertainties stemming from the monetary path of the United States (US) Federal Reserve and banking turmoil in the US and Europe.** Sustainable bond issuance in the region tallied USD47.7 billion in Q1 2023, recording a 13.8% q-o-q contraction after posting 2.7% q-o-q growth in Q4 2022. As a result, ASEAN+3's share of global sustainable bond issuance fell to 19.6% in Q1 2023 from 29.8% in Q4 2022 (**Figure 18**). Most regional markets saw reduced issuance of sustainable bonds during the quarter. While the People's Republic of China continued to lead the region in terms of sustainable bond issuance, it posted a 29.2% q-o-q contraction in Q1 2023, the largest decline among regional peers. The People's Republic of China accounted for a 45.9% share of ASEAN+3's sustainable bond issuance during the quarter, which was less than its 50.5% share of issuance in the region's overall bond market in the same period. Aggregate issuance in ASEAN markets declined by 27.7% q-o-q, resulting in its share of total regional bond issuance slipping to 5.8% in Q1 2023

from 6.9% in Q4 2022. In contrast, sustainable bond issuance in Hong Kong, China grew more than threefold in Q1 2023 to USD7.3 billion, buoyed by green bond issuance from the public sector in January.

**LCY issuance comprised a majority of ASEAN+3 sustainable bond issuance in Q1 2023 (Figure 19).** LCY issuance accounted for 61.7% of total sustainable

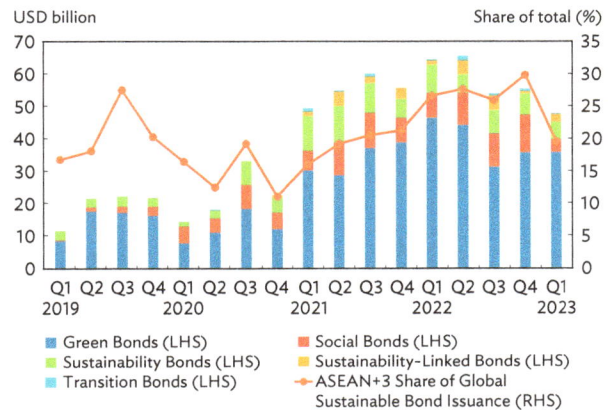

Figure 18: ASEAN+3 Sustainable Bond Issuance and Share of Global Sustainable Bond Issuance

ASEAN+3 = Association of Southeast Asian Nations plus the People's Republic of China; Hong Kong, China; Japan; and the Republic of Korea; LHS = left-hand side; Q1 = first quarter; Q2 = second quarter; Q3 = third quarter; Q4 = fourth quarter; RHS = right-hand side; USD = United States dollar.
Note: Data include both local currency and foreign currency issues.
Source: *AsianBondsOnline* calculations based on Bloomberg LP data.

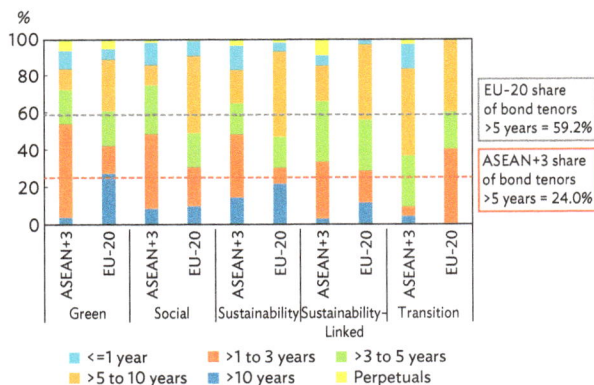

Figure 17: Maturity Profile of ASEAN+3 and EU-20 Sustainable Bonds Outstanding at the End of March 2023

ASEAN+3 = Association of Southeast Asian Nations plus the People's Republic of China; Hong Kong, China; Japan; and the Republic of Korea; EU = European Union.
Notes:
1. EU-20 includes EU member markets Austria, Belgium, Croatia, Cyprus, Estonia, Finland, France, Germany, Greece, Ireland, Italy, Latvia, Lithuania, Luxembourg, Malta, the Netherlands, Portugal, Slovakia, Slovenia, and Spain.
2. Data include both local currency and foreign currency issues.
Source: *AsianBondsOnline* calculations based on Bloomberg LP data.

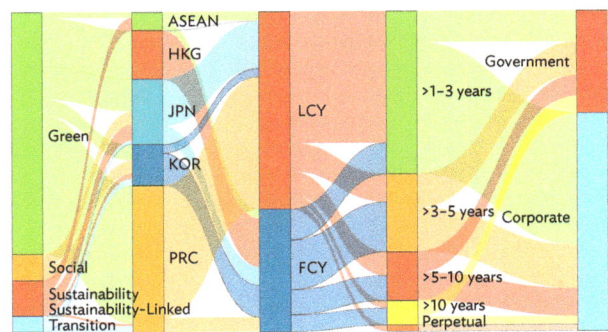

Figure 19: Market Profile of ASEAN+3 Sustainable Bond Issuance in the First Quarter of 2023

ASEAN = Association of Southeast Asian Nations; FCY = foreign currency; HKG = Hong Kong, China; JPN = Japan; KOR = Republic of Korea; LCY = local currency; PRC = People's Republic of China.
Notes:
1. ASEAN+3 is defined to include member states of ASEAN plus the People's Republic of China; Hong Kong, China; Japan; and the Republic of Korea.
2. ASEAN comprises the markets of Indonesia, Malaysia, the Philippines, Singapore, Thailand, and Viet Nam.
Source: *AsianBondsOnline* calculations based on Bloomberg LP data.

bond issuance in ASEAN+3 in Q1 2023. This was much lower than LCY bonds' dominant share of 94.6% in ASEAN+3's general bond issuance during the quarter. LCY issuance only accounted for 49.2% of total sustainable bond issuance in ASEAN markets. Of total LCY issuance in Q1 2023, 66.7% had a maturity of less than 3 years, while only 25.2% of foreign currency issuance was in the 1–3-year maturity basket. This implies that the ASEAN+3 sustainable bond market needs to strengthen the investor base for long-term LCY bonds.

**ASEAN+3's sustainable bond issuance in Q1 2023 was dominated by short-to medium-term tenors.**
Of the total sustainable bonds issued during the quarter, 75.0% carried maturities of 5 years or less. The size-weighted average maturity of ASEAN+3 sustainable bond issuance was 5.8 years in Q1 2023, a stark contrast with the size-weighted average maturity of 9.1 years in ASEAN+3's general bond market issuance in the same quarter. However, in ASEAN markets, more than 50% of sustainable bonds issued in Q1 2023 had tenors longer than 10 years. This was likely driven by a higher share of public sector issuance.

**Sustainable bond issuance in ASEAN+3 continued to be dominated by the private sector in Q1 2023.**
Sustainable bonds issued by the private sector accounted for 67.9% of the region's issuance total in Q1 2023, down from 76.2% in the prior quarter. In contrast, the private sector only accounted for a 28.0% share of the region's bond issuance total in Q1 2023. ASEAN sustainable bond markets had a relatively larger share of public sector issuance, comprising 45.4% of total sustainable bond issuance during the quarter. This, however, was still less than the public sector's 50.7% share of ASEAN's total bond issuance.

# Policy and Regulatory Developments

## People's Republic of China

### People's Bank of China Reduces Reserve Requirement Ratio

On 17 March, the People's Bank of China (PBOC) reduced the reserve requirement ratio for financial institutions by 25 basis points, effective 27 March. The cut, which brings the weighted-average reserve requirement ratio for financial institutions to around 7.6%, was taken to support economic recovery and provide adequate liquidity in the banking system.

## Hong Kong, China

### Hong Kong Monetary Authority Holds Countercyclical Capital Buffer Ratio at 1.0%

On 4 May, the Hong Kong Monetary Authority (HKMA) held the countercyclical buffer ratio steady at 1.0%. The HKMA noted that economic data as of the fourth quarter of 2022 showed a steady recovery of the domestic economy and indicated a countercyclical buffer ratio of 0.0%. However, the HKMA decided to hold the ratio unchanged at 1.0% given lingering uncertainties in the global economic environment. The countercyclical buffer ratio is an integral part of the Basel III regulatory capital framework intended to improve the resilience of the banking sector in periods of excess credit growth.

### Northbound Swap Connect Starts Operation

On 15 May, the PBOC, Hong Kong Securities and Futures Commission, and HKMA launched the Northbound channel of Swap Connect, a new mutual access program between the People's Republic of China (PRC) and Hong Kong, China's interbank interest rate swap markets. The program provides international investors access to the PRC's financial derivatives market through links established between financial institutions in the PRC and Hong Kong, China. By facilitating interest rate swaps, the program provides global investors in the PRC's bond market with a tool to manage interest rate risks. The initial daily trading quota for Swap Connect was set at CNY20.0 billion.

## Indonesia

### Government of Indonesia Sells the First Sovereign Blue Bonds in the World

On 19 May, the Government of Indonesia sold the first blue bonds issued by a sovereign entity. The blue bond sale comprised a 7-year and 10-year tranche denominated in Japanese yen with issue sizes of JPY14.7 billion and JPY6.0 billion, respectively. Blue bonds are bonds issued with the proceeds to be used to fund marine-related conservation initiatives and projects. The issuance is in line with the government's commitment to sustainable financing and efforts to diversify financing instruments and widen the investor base.

## Republic of Korea

### The Republic of Korea to Continue Institutional Reforms for Inclusion in the World Government Bond Index

On 30 March, FTSE Russell announced that the Republic of Korea would remain on the watch list for the World Government Bond Index after attaining first place on the list in September 2022. Market authorities in the Republic of Korea have undertaken and will continue to undertake institutional reforms to improve the structure and investor accessibility of the Republic of Korea's capital market. These include, among others, the exemption of withholding tax on Korea Treasury Bonds for foreign investors, abolishment of the Investment Registration Certificate scheme, and other foreign exchange (FX) market reforms. The inclusion in the World Government Bond Index is expected to increase foreign participation in the government bond market, balance market demand and supply, and improve market stability.

## Malaysia

### Malaysia Makes Cross-Border Payments Easy

In March and May, Bank Negara Malaysia, together with the Monetary Authority of Singapore (MAS) and Bank Indonesia, launched connected QR code payment systems between Singapore and Indonesia. Customers of participating Malaysian financial institutions can now scan Singapore's Network for Electronic Transfers QR codes and Indonesia's Quick Response Code Indonesian Standard to make retail payments. Likewise, customers of Singaporean and Indonesian institutions can make use of Malaysia's DuitNow QR codes. This improved connectivity promotes financial inclusion and upholds the Association of Southeast Asian Nations' goal of promoting connected retail payment systems in the region. The regional cooperation also benefits small- and medium-sized enterprises by boosting economic activities between markets and making it easier for consumers to settle in select local currencies.

## Philippines

### Bangko Sentral ng Pilipinas Revises Foreign Exchange Regulations

In its effort to streamline the procedures and documentary requirements for FX transactions, the Bangko Sentral ng Pilipinas (BSP) amended its FX regulations in March. Under the revised guidelines, the BSP permanently lifted the notarization requirement for certain supporting documents on trade and nontrade current account transactions as well as foreign investments. The BSP also waived the processing fee for noncompliance within the prescribed period for the submission of applications or requests for various FX transactions. Additionally, the BSP will continue to issue International Operations Department documents in electronic format and will permit authorized agent banks, their subsidiaries, and affiliated FX firms to receive BSP-issued documents via electronic means. The initiative aims to bolster economic integration with regional and global markets, as well as to enhance data capture for FX transactions.

## Singapore

### Singapore Strengthens Commitment to a Green Future

In April, the MAS launched its Finance for Net Zero Action Plan, which promotes financing geared toward decarbonization in Singapore's power generation and transportation industries, among others. The MAS plans to include transition bonds and loans in its sustainable bond and loan grant schemes. The central bank will ensure proper risk management in the lending activities mentioned, following international best practices.

Showing its commitment to a green future, the MAS and the PBOC launched a Green Finance Task Force in the same month. One of the aims of the group is to enhance the connectivity of the sustainable bond markets of Singapore and the PRC, allowing easy access to each market's green and transition bonds.

## Thailand

### Public Debt Management Office Plans THB40.0 Billion Issuance of Savings Bonds

On 27 April, the Government of Thailand's Public Debt Management Office announced a triple-tranche offering of savings bonds amounting to THB40.0 billion and with a subscription period of 10–23 May. The first tranche worth THB10.0 billion was accessible to retail investors through Krungthai Bank's Sasom Bond Mung Kung e-wallet. The second tranche worth THB25.0 billion was also open to individual investors through dealer banks (e.g., Bangkok Bank, Krungthai Bank, Kasikorn Bank, and Siam Commercial Bank) via mobile banking or over-the-counter transactions. The final tranche worth THB5.0 billion was made available to nonprofit organizations at the counters of dealer banks. The planned savings bond issuance aims to help finance the government's budget deficit for fiscal year 2023 and follows the record issuance of THB46.1 billion worth of savings bonds in December 2022.

# Viet Nam

## Corporate Bond Regulations Amended

Due to various challenges faced by corporate bond issuers since the implementation of Decree No. 65 in September 2022, coupled with the recent turmoil in the domestic real estate market, the Government of Viet Nam issued Decree No. 8 on 5 March. The new decree aims to amend and suspend several provisions stipulated in Decree No. 65, and loosens the government's restrictions on corporate bond regulations to help ease pressure on corporate bond issuers. Decree No. 8 allows issuers to negotiate with bondholders and extends payments by a maximum of 2 years if holders agree. It also allows issuers to make payments by assets other than cash for domestically issued bonds and suspends the requirements for professional investor status and credit ratings to 1 January 2024. Furthermore, the previous rule on a 30-day distribution period for each private placement has been postponed until the end of 2023. The new regulations provide issuers with additional time to encourage investment, increasing the likelihood of a successful bond offering.

# Climate Risk Awareness and Fund Trading of Individual Investors

Public awareness of climate change has increased significantly during the past decade. Dechezleprêtre et al. (2022) surveyed more than 40,000 respondents in 20 countries that account for 72% of global $CO_2$ emissions and found that "at least 75% of respondents in each country agree that 'climate change is an important problem' and that their country 'should take measures to fight it.'"[6]

Increased awareness of climate-related risks could affect investment decisions toward green assets via two possible ways: (i) the adjusted expectation for future cash flows on green vs. brown assets (i.e., financial motives), (ii) the change in investor preferences for sustainability (i.e., nonfinancial motives) (Pastor, Stambaugh, and Taylor 2020). As governments worldwide introduce various policies to mitigate climate change, institutional investors are incorporating climate-related risks into their investment decisions for both financial and nonfinancial motives (Pastor, Stambaugh, and Taylor 2020; Krueger, Sautner, and Starks 2020; Alok, Kumar, and Wermers 2020; Bolton and Kacperczyk 2021). However, evidence of whether individual investors consider climate-related risks in their investment decisions remains thin. This study contributes to current knowledge by providing evidence on how climate risk awareness affects individual investment decisions. Utilizing account-level data of individuals in the People's Republic of China (PRC), this study investigates whether climate risk awareness affects individual investors' trading and investment decisions toward environmental, social, and governance (ESG) assets.

The literature suggests that governments' environmental commitments are likely to raise investors' climate risk awareness. For instance, Bolton and Kacperczyk (2021) use the Paris Agreement as a shock to investors' awareness about carbon risk and show that the carbon premium increased following the signing of the agreement. To clearly identify the role of increased climate risk awareness, the study uses the PRC's announcement of dual carbon targets (DCT) to proxy an exogenous shock to investors' climate risk awareness. In September 2020, at the 75th United Nations General Assembly, the PRC proposed its DCT, setting the goals of reaching a $CO_2$ emissions peak by 2030 and carbon neutrality by 2060. It is thus expected that the PRC's DCT announcement would have boosted Chinese investors' awareness of climate-related risks. Focusing on individual investors' trading of ESG mutual funds, it is anticipated that individual investors would have increased their portfolio exposure to ESG mutual funds after the announcement of DCT due to increased climate risk awareness.

The study uses a sample of 200,000 randomly selected individual investors from the online mutual fund investment platform on Alipay, which is currently the largest third-party mobile and online payment platform in the PRC. The platform is operated by the fintech giant, Ant Group. The sample consists of monthly mutual fund trading data for individual investors from October 2019 to September 2021. The sample period spans from 1 year before to 1 year after September 2020, when the PRC first announced its DCT.

For each individual investor $i$ in month $t$, the net purchase of a mutual fund $j$ in investor $i$'s portfolio is calculated as the difference between the total purchase and the redemption of fund $j$ scaled by the sum of the two. The key dependent variable, $NetPurchase_{i,j,t}$, thus conveys information on investor $i$'s trading of $j$ at time $t$. A higher value for this variable indicates investor $i$'s increased investment and interest in mutual fund $j$ in month $t$. Since the PRC's announcement of DCT is used as a shock to investors' climate risk awareness, September 2020, when the targets were first proposed, is set as the even month. A dummy variable, $Post_t$, is given a value of 1 for sample

---

[6]  This summary was prepared based on findings in the working paper written by Zhenyu Gao, Yan Luo, Shu Tian, and Hao Yang, previously circulated under the name "Climate Risk Awareness and Investment Decisions: Individual-Level Evidence from the People's Republic of China."

months after the even month and 0 otherwise. A mutual fund $j$ in month $t$ is labeled as an ESG fund if it is included among the ESG Theme Funds of WIND, a leading financial data service provider in the PRC. A dummy variable, $ESG_{j,t}$, is given a value of 1 if a mutual fund $j$ is an ESG fund at time $t$ and 0 otherwise.

To examine whether individual investors' trading of ESG funds was influenced by increased climate risk awareness after the PRC's DCT announcement in September 2020, the study performs investor-fund-month level regressions. Investor $i$'s net purchase of fund $j$ in month $t$ is regressed on an interaction term, $Post_t * ESG_{j,t}$, where $Post_t$ is equal to 1 after the even month and $ESG_{j,t}$ is an indicator of ESG funds. To account for possible factors that would affect individual investment decisions, individual-, fund-, and time-fixed effects are controlled for in the analysis. To account for investment decisions that could be driven by fund performance, the mutual fund's performance during the prior 3 months and subsequent 3 months are also controlled for. The results are reported in **Table 3**.

As shown, the results indicate a significant increase in individual investors' net purchase of ESG mutual funds compared to non-ESG mutual funds after the PRC's announcement of DCT. The results are robust when various fixed effects have been included and fund returns over the previous 3 months and subsequent 3 months have been controlled for, suggesting that the results are not purely driven by the features of individuals, fund performance or time, nor by changes in information that are related to fund performances around the event. Such findings are consistent with current knowledge on institutional investors. This study indicates that governments' climate commitments and policies can drive resource allocation, not only via incentives and regulation but also by shaping investors' risk appetite and investment behavior. Policies that effectively guide investment decisions can help cost-efficiently mobilize capital toward ESG investments.

**Table 3: Individual Investors' ESG Fund Trading after the PRC's DCT Announcement**

| Variable | (1) $NetPurchase_{i,j,t}$ | (2) $NetPurchase_{i,j,t}$ | (3) $NetPurchase_{i,j,t}$ | (4) $NetPurchase_{i,j,t}$ |
|---|---|---|---|---|
| $Post_t * ESG_{j,t}$ | 0.0539*** (23.176) | 0.0639*** (27.436) | 0.0465*** (19.957) | 0.059*** (25.23) |
| $Fund\ Return_{j,t-1}$ | | 0.0047*** (65.765) | | 0.0046*** (60.212) |
| $Fund\ Return_{j,t-2}$ | | 0.0001 (1.5451) | | 0.0002*** (2.8135) |
| $Fund\ Return_{j,t-3}$ | | 0.0036*** (40.815) | | 0.0035*** (38.45) |
| $Fund\ Return_{j,t+1}$ | | | −0.0022*** (−28.902) | −0.0004*** (−5.0451) |
| $Fund\ Return_{j,t+2}$ | | | 0.0003*** (3.7087) | 0.0003*** (4.0626) |
| $Fund\ Return_{j,t+3}$ | | | −0.0027*** (−34.376) | −0.0021*** (−26.79) |
| Investor fixed effects | YES | YES | YES | YES |
| Fund fixed effects | YES | YES | YES | YES |
| Month fixed effects | YES | YES | YES | YES |
| Adj. $R_2$ | 0.1188 | 0.1203 | 0.1193 | 0.1205 |
| No. of Obs. | 3371729 | 3371729 | 3371729 | 3371729 |

DCT = dual carbon targets; ESG = environmental, social, and governance; PRC = People's Republic of China.
Note: Robust t-statistics are reported in parentheses. *, **, and *** represent significance at the 10%, 5%, and 1% levels, respectively.
Source: Authors' estimates.

## References

Alok, Shashwat, Nitin Kumar, and Russ Wermers. 2020. "Do Fund Managers Misestimate Climatic disaster Risk?" *Review of Financial Studies* 33 (3): 1146–83.

Bolton, Patrick, and Marcin Kacperczyk. 2021. "Do Investors Care about Carbon Risk?" *Journal of Financial Economics* 142 (2): 517–49.

Dechezleprêtre, Antoine, Caterina Gennaioli, Ralf Martin, Mirabelle Muûls, and Thomas Stoerk. 2022. "Searching for Carbon Leaks in Multinational Companies." *Journal of Environmental Economics and Management* 112 (2022): 102601.

Krueger, Philipp, Zacharias Sautner, and Laura T. Starks. 2020. "The Importance of Climate Risks for Institutional Investors." *The Review of Financial Studies* 33 (3): 1067–111.

Pastor, Lubos, Robert Stambaugh, and Lucian Taylor. 2020. "Sustainable Investing in Equilibrium." *Journal of Financial Economics* 142 (2020): 550–71.

# Market Summaries

## People's Republic of China

### Yield Movements

Between 1 March and 2 June, local currency (LCY) government bond yields in the People's Republic of China (PRC) fell for all maturities except tenors of less than 1 year, which rose slightly, and the 8-year and 9-year tenors, which were unchanged (**Figure 1**). Yields for all remaining tenors showed a strong decline, particularly longer tenors, over economic growth concerns in the PRC. While sentiment was initially positive in 2023, concerns that the growth momentum may be fading have since risen. Gross domestic product growth accelerated in the first quarter (Q1) of 2023 to 4.5% year-on-year (y-o-y) from 2.9% y-o-y in the fourth quarter (Q4) of 2022. But concerns over the sustainability of the economic recovery increased after industrial production and retail sales growth in April came in lower than expected. Declining yields were also influenced by the People's Bank of China's cut in the reserve requirement ratio for financial institutions by 25 basis points, effective 27 March, to support economic growth. The government also announced that it would develop measures to boost the property sector. In June, the central bank reduced by 10 basis points each the 7-day reverse repurchase rate and the 1-year medium-term lending facility rate.

### Local Currency Bond Market Size and Issuance

**The PRC continued to dominate the LCY bond market in emerging East Asia.** LCY bonds outstanding in the PRC reached CNY130.3 trillion (USD19.0 trillion) at the end of March, representing 79.8% of the regional bond market. Growth quickened to 2.3% quarter-on-quarter (q-o-q) in Q1 2023 from 1.3% q-o-q in Q4 2022 as issuance rebounded during the quarter (**Figure 2**). Much of the growth came from Treasury and other government bonds, which were buoyed by the frontloading of local governments' annual bond quotas at the start of the year. Treasury and other government bonds accounted for a 65.9% share of the PRC's overall LCY bond market at the end of March, while corporate bonds had a 34.1% share. As a share of regional markets, the PRC's bonds outstanding comprised 84.8% of Treasury and other government bonds and 76.0% of corporate bonds at the end of March.

**LCY bond sales in the PRC totaled CNY10.1 trillion in Q1 2023, accounting for 63.1% of emerging East Asia's issuance total during the quarter.** Issuance of Treasury

### Figure 1: The People's Republic of China's Benchmark Yield Curve—Local Currency Government Bonds

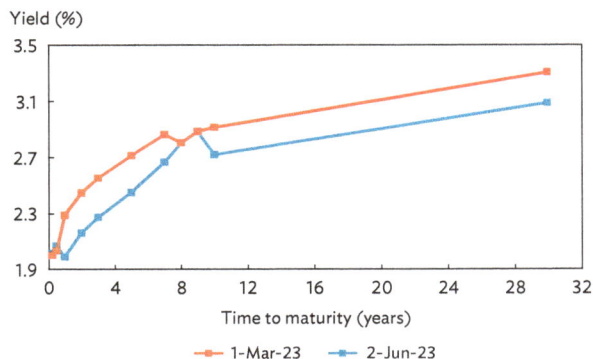

Yield (%)

Time to maturity (years)

— 1-Mar-23   — 2-Jun-23

Source: Based on data from Bloomberg LP.

### Figure 2: Composition of Local Currency Bonds Outstanding in the People's Republic of China

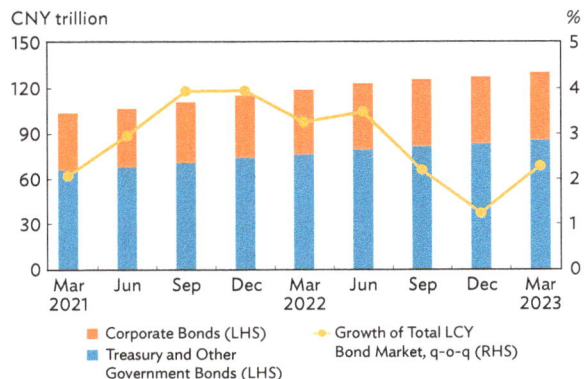

CNY trillion   %

■ Corporate Bonds (LHS)
■ Treasury and Other Government Bonds (LHS)
— Growth of Total LCY Bond Market, q-o-q (RHS)

CNY = Chinese yuan, LCY = local currency, LHS = left-hand side, q-o-q = quarter-on-quarter, RHS = right-hand side.
Source: CEIC Data Company.

and other government bonds climbed 10.8% q-o-q in Q1 2023, after contracting 6.8% q-o-q in Q4 2022, to reach CNY5.9 trillion (**Figure 3**). In line with measures to prop up the economy, the bond quota for issuing local government bonds in 2023 was announced at the start of the year; local governments were authorized to issue bonds amounting to CNY3.8 trillion beginning in January. Meanwhile, corporate bond issuance contracted at a slower pace of 0.6% q-o-q in Q1 2023 versus 6.5% q-o-q

in the prior quarter. Among corporate bond types, commercial paper posted the largest uptick during the quarter, rising 27.2% q-o-q from a 7.6% q-o-q decline in Q4 2022 (**Figure 4**). Issuance of listed corporate enterprise bonds and medium-term notes accelerated in Q1 2023 versus Q4 2023, while issuance of financial bonds and asset-backed securities slowed during the same period. The largest corporate bond issuances during the quarter came from the Bank of Communications, Industrial Bank, and Agricultural Bank of China. Most corporate bond issuances in Q1 2023 were from financial institutions as they beefed up funding for their lending activities.

## Investor Profile

**Among domestic investors, commercial banks remained the largest holder of government bonds at the end of March** (**Figure 5**). Commercial banks were the largest holder of government bonds at the end of March with a total share of 73.1%, slightly higher than their share of 71.1% a year earlier. Commercial banks also held the largest share of local government bonds at the end of March with 85.7%.

### Figure 3: Composition of Local Currency Bond Issuance in the People's Republic of China

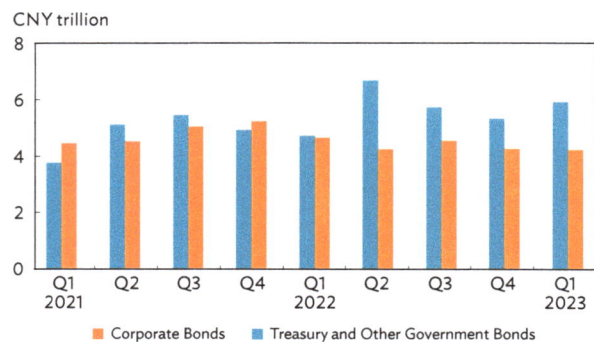

CNY = Chinese yuan, Q1 = first quarter, Q2 = second quarter, Q3 = third quarter, Q4 = fourth quarter.
Source: CEIC Data Company.

### Figure 4: Corporate Bond Issuance Breakdown

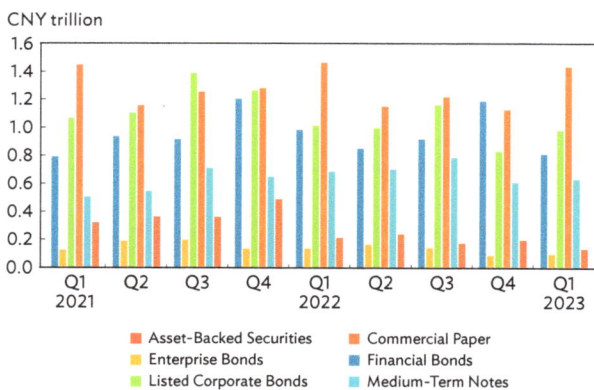

CNY = Chinese yuan, Q1 = first quarter, Q2 = second quarter, Q3 = third quarter, Q4 = fourth quarter.
Source: CEIC Data Company.

### Figure 5: Investor Profile of Local Government Bonds, Policy Bank Bonds, and Treasury Bonds

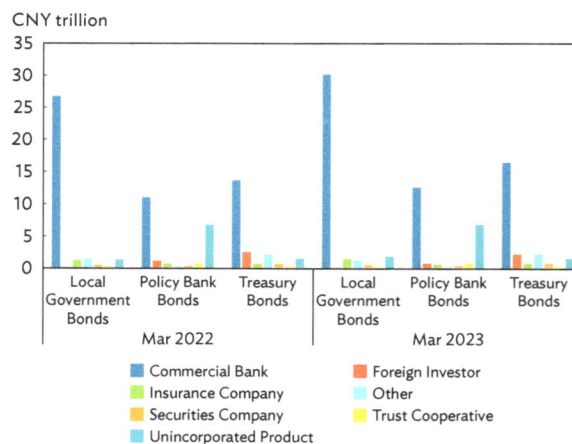

CNY = Chinese yuan.
Source: CEIC Data Company.

# Hong Kong, China

## Yield Movements

**Hong Kong, China's local currency (LCY) government bond yields showed mixed movements between 1 March and 2 June.** Yields jumped at the short-end but rose for all tenors longer than 1 year (**Figure 1**). The rise at the short end of the yield curve reflected tightened liquidity conditions. Several interventions by the Hong Kong Monetary Authority (HKMA) to defend the Hong Kong dollar's peg to the United States (US) dollar drained liquidity from the banking system. The aggregate balance—a measure of interbank liquidity—was down to HKD44.8 billion on 2 June from HKD77.0 billion on 1 March. The uptick in short-term bond yields was also influenced by the rise in the HKMA's policy rate. The HKMA adjusts its base rate in line with the US Federal Reserve's policy rate decisions to maintain the Hong Kong dollar's peg to the US dollar. On 4 May, the HKMA increased its base rate by 25 basis points to 5.50% after the Federal Reserve raised the target range for its policy rate by a quarter percentage point to a range of 5.00% to 5.25%. Meanwhile, the decline in yields for tenors longer than 1 year largely tracked yield movements of US Treasuries, which fell amid expectations that the Federal Reserve would pause its monetary policy tightening during its June meeting.

## Local Currency Bond Market Size and Issuance

**Hong Kong, China's LCY bond market reached a size of HKD2.8 trillion (USD356.9 billion) at the end of March.** Total LCY bonds outstanding rose 1.1% quarter-on-quarter (q-o-q) in the first quarter (Q1) of 2023, up from 0.8% q-o-q in the preceding quarter (**Figure 2**). Growth was largely driven by the corporate bond segment, which expanded faster in Q1 2023 amid the recovery of the domestic economy. Hong Kong, China's gross domestic product rebounded, rising 2.7% year-on-year in Q1 2023 after recording 4 quarters of contraction in 2022. Corporate bonds dominated the LCY bond market, with the outstanding corporate bond stock of HKD1.4 trillion comprising 48.5% of total LCY bonds at the end of March. Exchange Fund Bills and Exchange Fund Notes together accounted for 43.4% of total LCY bonds, while Hong Kong Special Administrative Region (HKSAR) bonds had a smaller share of 8.1%. Exchange Fund Bills and Exchange Fund Notes are utilized as liquidity management instruments, hence their relatively larger share in Hong Kong, China's bond market.

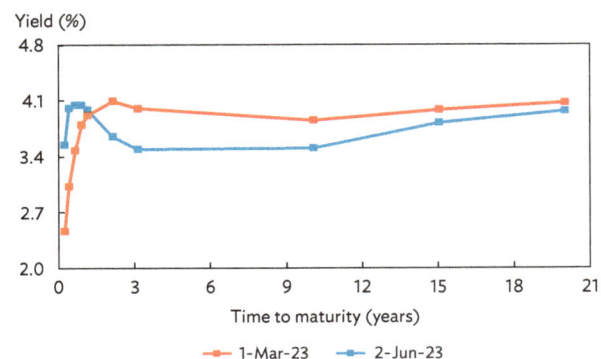

**Figure 1: Hong Kong, China's Benchmark Yield Curve—Exchange Fund Bills and Notes**

Yield (%)

— 1-Mar-23  — 2-Jun-23

Source: Based on data from Bloomberg LP.

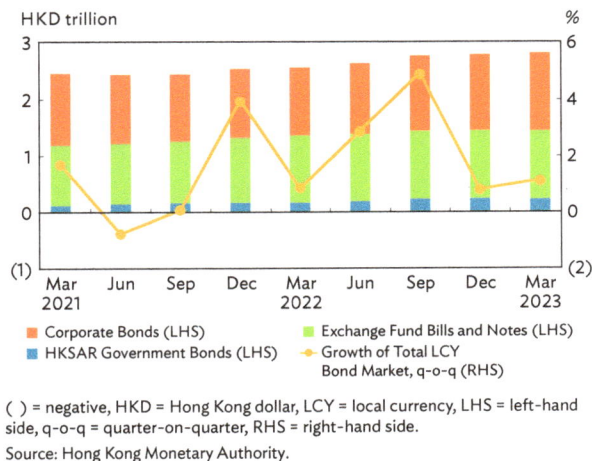

**Figure 2: Composition of Local Currency Bonds Outstanding in Hong Kong, China**

HKD trillion / %

Corporate Bonds (LHS)
HKSAR Government Bonds (LHS)
Exchange Fund Bills and Notes (LHS)
Growth of Total LCY Bond Market, q-o-q (RHS)

( ) = negative, HKD = Hong Kong dollar, LCY = local currency, LHS = left-hand side, q-o-q = quarter-on-quarter, RHS = right-hand side.
Source: Hong Kong Monetary Authority.

**New issuance of LCY bonds jumped 7.8% q-o-q to HKD1.3 trillion in Q1 2023.** Growth in HKSAR bond issuance rebounded, rising 30.0% q-o-q in Q1 2023 after posting an 87.8% q-o-q contraction in the prior quarter (**Figure 3**). HKSAR government bonds issued in Q1 2023 tallied HKD7.8 billion, including HKD0.8 billion of

institutional green bonds and HKD1.5 billion of floating-rate notes indexed to the Hong Kong Dollar Overnight Index Average.

**The world's first tokenized government green bonds were issued in Hong Kong, China in February.** A total of HKD0.8 billion worth of 365-day government green bonds were issued using distributed ledger technology, which shortened the settlement cycle. The same technology will be applied for the bond's coupon payment, settlement of secondary trading, and maturity redemption. The landmark issuance was part of Hong Kong, China's initiatives to promote innovation in financial technology and green and sustainable finance.

**Issuance of corporate debt totaled HKD278.1 billion in Q1 2022, rising 43.3% q-o-q in Q1 2023 after contracting 19.7% q-o-q in the preceding quarter.** The reopening of borders with the People's Republic of China and the return of business activities revived investor confidence and boosted demand for corporate bonds in Q1 2023. The largest nonbank corporate bond issuer was Hong Kong Mortgage Corporation with total issuances amounting to HKD28.2 billion in Q1 2023.

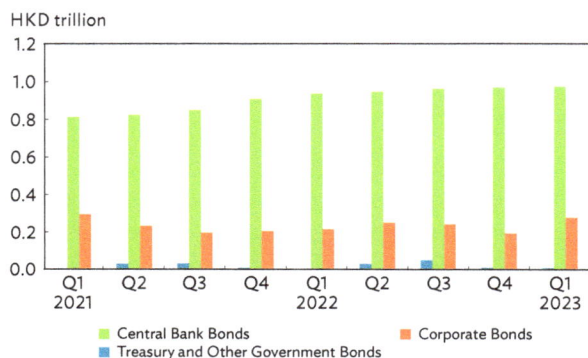

**Figure 3: Composition of Local Currency Bond Issuance in Hong Kong, China**

HKD trillion

Legend:
- Central Bank Bonds
- Treasury and Other Government Bonds
- Corporate Bonds

HKD = Hong Kong dollar, Q1 = first quarter, Q2 = second quarter, Q3 = third quarter, Q4 = fourth quarter.
Source: Hong Kong Monetary Authority.

# Indonesia

## Yield Movements

**Local currency (LCY) government bond yields in Indonesia declined for all maturities from 1 March to 2 June, resulting in the yield curve's shift downward (Figure 1).** Bond yields trended down as Bank Indonesia held steady its 7-day reverse repurchase rate at 5.75% for a fourth straight month in May after raising rates by a cumulative 225 basis points from August 2022 to January 2023, as inflation gradually declined. Consumer price inflation slipped to 4.0% year-on-year in May from 4.3% year-on-year in April, hitting the central bank's target range of 2.0%–4.0% for 2023 earlier than expected. The central bank had previously forecasted inflation to return to its target range by the third quarter of 2023. Declining yields were also fueled by expectations that the United States (US) Federal Reserve would hold rates steady in its June Federal Open Market Committee meeting. Investors were pricing a 74.7% chance of a pause in monetary tightening by the US Federal Reserve, based on the CME FedWatch Tool, as of 2 June.

### Figure 1: Indonesia's Benchmark Yield Curve—Local Currency Government Bonds

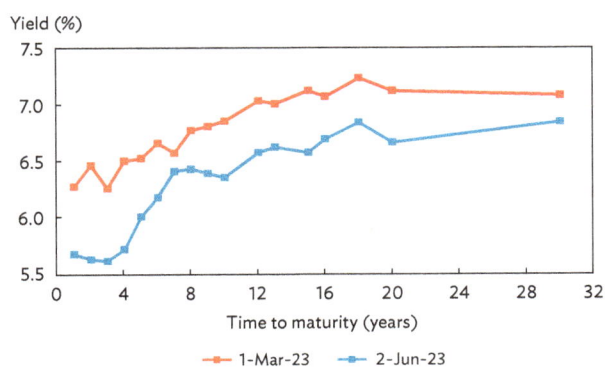

Source: Based on data from Bloomberg LP.

## Local Currency Bond Market Size and Issuance

**LCY bonds outstanding in Indonesia reached IDR6,161.1 trillion (USD410.9 billion) at the end of March.** Overall bond market growth was steady at 3.5% quarter-on-quarter (q-o-q) in the first quarter (Q1) of 2023 (**Figure 2**). Growth was largely driven by Treasury and other government bonds as the government continued to adopt a frontloading policy for the issuance

### Figure 2: Composition of Local Currency Bonds Outstanding in Indonesia

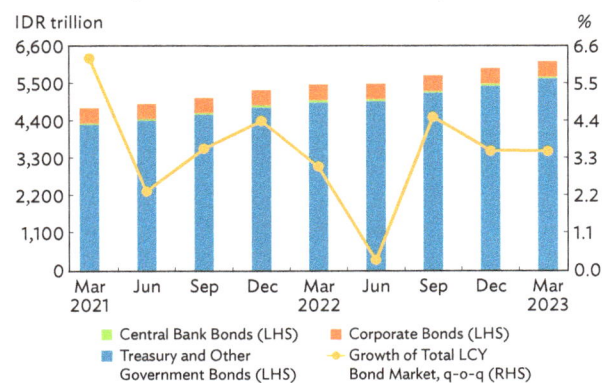

IDR = Indonesian rupiah, LCY = local currency, LHS = left-hand side, q-o-q = quarter-on-quarter, RHS = right-hand side.
Note: Data includes *sukuk* (Islamic bonds). Data for Treasury and other government bonds comprised of tradable and nontradable central government bonds.
Sources: Bank Indonesia; Directorate General of Budget Financing and Risk Management, Ministry of Finance; and Indonesia Stock Exchange.

of Treasury bonds during the first half of the year. Treasury and other government bonds dominate Indonesia's LCY bond market, accounting for 91.8% of total bonds outstanding at the end of March, the highest share among its emerging East Asian peers. In contrast, Indonesia's corporate bonds account for only 7.3% of the total LCY bond market, the smallest LCY corporate bond market in the region by share of the overall market.

**Total LCY bond issuance reached IDR544.1 trillion in the first quarter (Q1) of 2023, as issuance of Treasury bonds rebounded.** Issuance of Treasury bonds totaled IDR245.4 trillion on modest growth of 2.2% q-o-q, a reversal from the 10.3% q-o-q contraction in the fourth quarter of 2022 (**Figure 3**). In addition to weekly Treasury auctions, the government raised a total of IDR22.2 trillion from its offering of Savings Bond Ritel, a nontradable retail savings bond for Indonesian citizens. The bonds comprised a 2-year and a 4-year tranche and were structured to provide individuals with a short- to medium-term investment option. Meanwhile, corporate bond issuance tallied IDR27.5 trillion in Q1 2023, up by 1.8% q-o-q. The largest corporate bond issuers during the quarter were Federal International Finance and Professional Telekomunikasi Indonesia, with total issuances of IDR3.0 trillion and IDR2.9 trillion, respectively.

**Sukuk (Islamic bonds) account for a relatively small share of Indonesia's LCY bond market.** The overall

### Figure 3: Composition of Local Currency Bond Issuance in Indonesia

IDR trillion

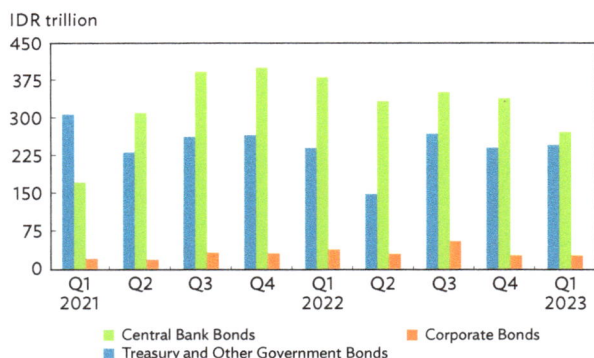

IDR = Indonesian rupiah, Q1 = first quarter, Q2 = second quarter, Q3 = third quarter, Q4 = fourth quarter.

Note: Data includes *sukuk* (Islamic bonds). Data for Treasury and other government bonds comprise tradable and nontradable central government bonds.

Sources: Bank Indonesia; Directorate General of Budget Financing and Risk Management, Ministry of Finance; and Indonesia Stock Exchange.

amount of *sukuk* outstanding in Indonesia reached IDR1,172.0 trillion at the end of March, which is equivalent to a 19.0% share of the total LCY bond market size (**Figure 4**). The *sukuk* market, however, saw substantial gains from a size of only IDR37.0 trillion in March 2013. By market segment, Treasury *sukuk* accounted for a 19.0% share of total Treasury bonds outstanding, while corporate *sukuk* comprised an even smaller share of 9.6% of the corporate bonds outstanding by the end of March 2023.

## Investor Profile

**Among domestic investors, central bank holdings gained the most, accounting for an 18.3% share of total central government bonds at the end of March.** Since the pandemic, Bank Indonesia has beefed up its holdings of Treasury bonds to support bond

### Figure 4: *Sukuk* Outstanding

IDR trillion

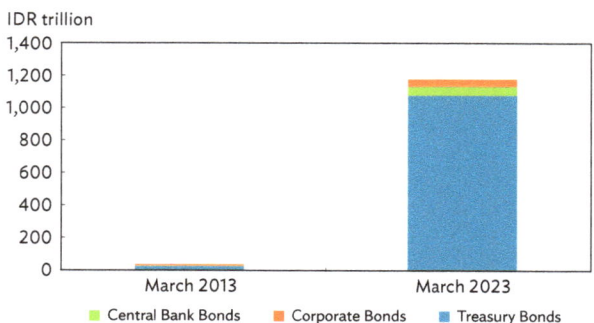

IDR = Indonesian rupiah, *sukuk* = Islamic bonds.

Sources: Bank Indonesia; Directorate General of Budget Financing and Risk Management, Ministry of Finance; and Indonesia Stock Exchange.

market stability. In contrast, bank holdings of central government bonds declined, with its holdings' share falling to 31.9% at the end of March 2023 from 35.0% a year earlier. Nonetheless, banks remained the largest investor in both conventional and Islamic bonds at the end of Q1 2023 (**Figure 5**). The foreign holdings' share also dipped to 14.9% amid aggressive monetary rate hikes by the Federal Reserve, which led to capital outflows from the Indonesian bond market for most of 2022. While capital inflows were recorded in Q1 2023, they were more than offset by the capital outflows in the prior year. Holdings of offshore investors remained concentrated in medium- to longer-term tenors at the end of March (**Figure 6**). Bonds with maturities of over 5 years to 10 years accounted for a 45.9% share of foreign holdings, while bonds with tenors of over 10 years had a 23.7% share.

### Figure 5: Investor Profile of Tradable Central Government Bonds

IDR trillion

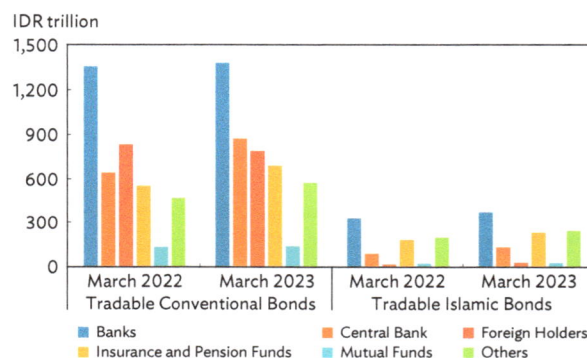

IDR = Indonesian rupiah.

Source: Directorate General of Budget Financing and Risk Management, Ministry of Finance.

### Figure 6: Foreign Holdings of Local Currency Tradable Central Government Bonds by Maturity at the End of March 2023

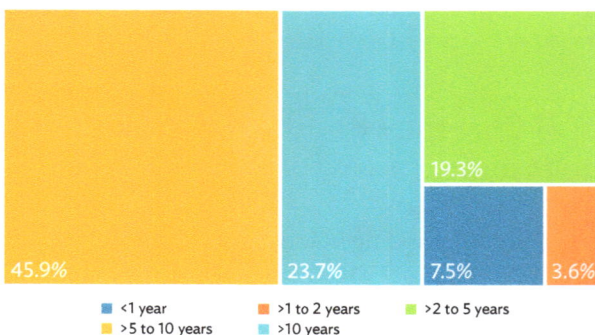

IDR = Indonesian rupiah.

Source: Directorate General of Budget Financing and Risk Management, Ministry of Finance.

# Republic of Korea

## Yield Movements

**The Republic of Korea's local currency (LCY) government bond yield curve flattened between 1 March and 2 June, with the drop in yields most pronounced for medium-term bonds (Figure 1).** Bond yields fell due to the Bank of Korea's decision to maintain the base rate at 3.50% in its monetary policy meetings in April and May, amid slowing inflation and economic growth and on increased expectations that the US Federal Reserve would hold rates steady in its June monetary policy meeting.

Yields fell sharply for all tenors in March, with tenors between 1-year and 10-year posting the largest declines, as they tracked the decline in United States (US) Treasury yields following the collapse of Silicon Valley Bank. However, in April, domestic bond yields remained range-bound amid easing concerns over the US banking system and as market participants awaited further signals from the Federal Reserve on the timing as to the end of the rate-hike cycle (**Figure 2**). Also in April, the Bank of Korea maintained the base rate at 3.50%, as both inflation and economic growth were observed to have slowed. Subsequently, in its 25 May monetary policy meeting, the Bank of Korea again maintained the base rate; and lowered its 2023 and 2024 growth forecasts to 1.4% year-on-year (y-o-y) and 2.3% y-o-y, respectively, from January forecasts of 1.6% y-o-y and 2.4% y-o-y. Meanwhile, the inflation forecast for 2023

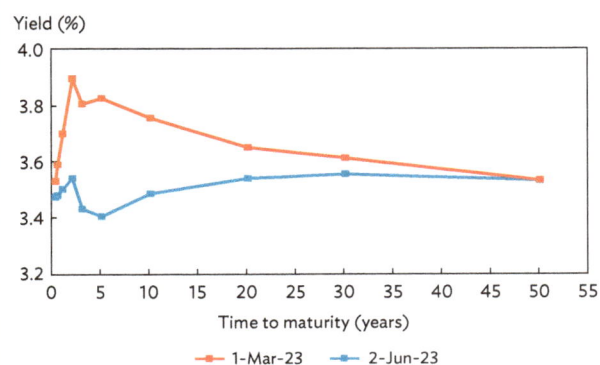

**Figure 2: Local Currency Government Bond Yields— Selected Tenors**

Note: Data coverage is from 1 March to 2 June 2023.
Source: Based on data from Bloomberg LP.

was maintained at 3.5%, while for 2024 it was lowered to 2.4% from 2.6%. In May, domestic bond yields started to pick up again, largely for the short- and long-term bonds tracking the rise in US Treasury yields, as market participants awaited the result of the debt ceiling deal negotiations in the US.

## Local Currency Bond Market Size and Issuance

**The Republic of Korea's LCY bond market reached a size of KRW3,014.2 trillion (USD2.3 trillion) at the end of March.** Overall growth accelerated to 1.5% quarter-on-quarter (q-o-q) in the first quarter (Q1) of 2023 from 0.1% q-o-q in the previous quarter, and was mainly driven by the 1.3% q-o-q increase in the stock of corporate bonds. Meanwhile, the stock of Treasury and other government bonds rose at a slightly slower pace of 1.2% q-o-q on increased issuance during the quarter. Corporate bonds continued to comprise 57.4% of the Republic of Korea's LCY bond market at the end of March, declining somewhat from a share of 58.4% at the end of Q1 2021 (**Figure 3**). Meanwhile, the share of Treasury and other government bonds had been steadily increasing to 38.5% at the end of March.

**LCY bond issuance rose 4.7% q-o-q to KRW247.2 trillion in Q1 2023.** Growth was largely driven by the increase in issuance of Treasury and other government bonds as corporate bond issuance fell during the quarter (**Figure 4**).

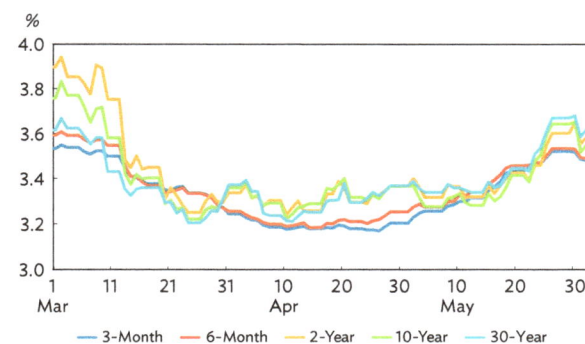

**Figure 1: The Republic of Korea's Benchmark Yield Curve—Local Currency Government Bonds**

Source: Based on data from Bloomberg LP.

**Figure 3: Composition of Local Currency Bonds Outstanding in the Republic of Korea**

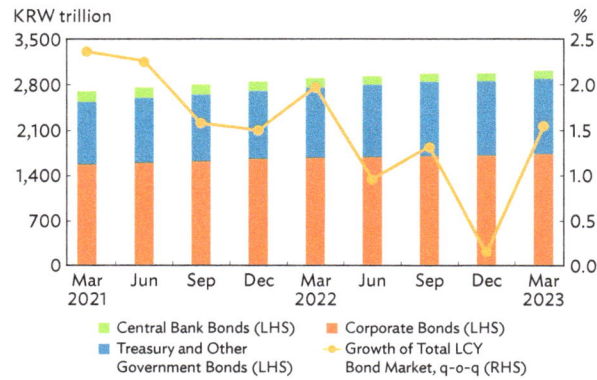

KRW = Korean won, LCY = local currency, LHS = left-hand side, q-o-q = quarter-on-quarter, RHS = right-hand side.
Sources: Bank of Korea and KG Zeroin Corp.

**Figure 4: Composition of Local Currency Bond Issuance in the Republic of Korea**

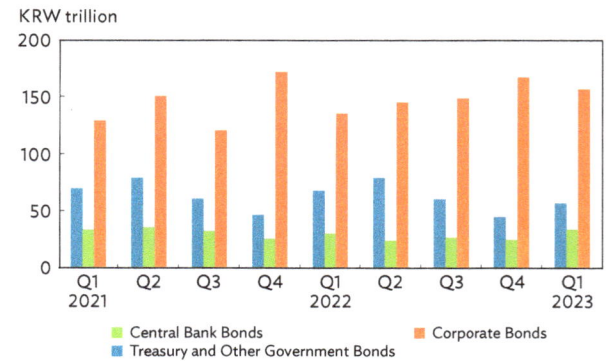

KRW = Korean won, Q1 = first quarter, Q2 = second quarter, Q3 = third quarter, Q4 = fourth quarter.
Sources: Bank of Korea and KG Zeroin Corp.

Issuance of Treasury and other government bonds rose 27.2% q-o-q, in line with the frontloading policy of the Government of the Republic of Korea, under which it plans to release 65% of its 2023 budget in the first half of the year.

**Half of all outstanding corporate bonds comprised bonds issued by private companies at the end of March, while financial debentures and special public bonds accounted for a quarter share each.** Total corporate bond issuance in Q1 2023 fell 6.2% q-o-q, led by the decline in issuances from private companies and financial institutions; only special public bonds posted a q-o-q increase in Q1 2023 (**Figure 5**). The quarterly decline

was mostly due to a high base of issuances from private companies in December 2022 as firms refinanced their maturing debts. One of the notable corporate bond issuances in Q1 2023 included the KRW1,210 trillion 3-year and 5-year bond issuances by SK hynix, the second-largest memory chipmaker in the world.

## Investor Profile

**Insurance companies and pension funds continued to be among the largest investor groups in the Republic of Korea's LCY bond market.** In the government bond segment, insurance companies and pension funds held the largest share at the end of

**Figure 5: Composition of Local Currency Corporate Bonds Outstanding and Issuance in the Republic of Korea**

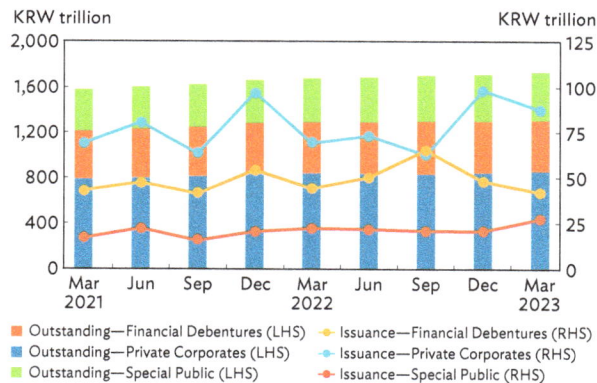

KRW = Korean won, LHS = left-hand side, RHS = right-hand side.
Source: KG Zeroin Corp.

**Figure 6: Local Currency Bonds Outstanding Investor Profile**

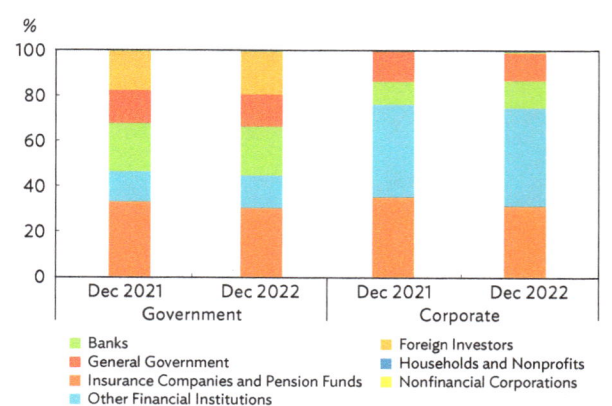

Sources: AsianBondsOnline and Bank of Korea.

December 2022 with 30.4% of the total (**Figure 6**). Banks and foreign investors followed with shares of 21.7% and 19.1%, respectively. In the Republic of Korea's LCY corporate bond market, insurance companies and pension fund holdings' share of 31.5% was second to that of other financial institutions at 43.3%. The foreign holdings of domestic corporate bonds remained negligible at the end of December 2022.

**Aggregate net foreign flows into the Republic of Korea's LCY bond market remained negative in Q1 2023.** A record KRW6.6 trillion of net foreign outflows was registered in January, with foreign investors selling and taking profits on their short-term investments, as short-term yields dropped during the month following an upward trend in 2022. The bulk of the foreign selling in January was in securities with tenors of less than 1 year (**Figure 7**). Net foreign outflows continued in February but at a smaller amount of KRW0.8 trillion, as net buying of long-term bonds increased, nearly offsetting the selling in short-term and medium-term bonds. This trend was reversed in March, with the domestic bond market posting net inflows of KRW3.1 trillion, the highest net inflows since July 2022. Foreign demand rose in March on increased expectations that the Bank of Korea would start cutting interest rates this year as inflation decelerates, providing an upside to foreign investors. However, the net foreign inflows in March were not enough to offset the massive net outflows in January, resulting in aggregate net foreign outflows of KRW4.3 trillion in Q1 2023.

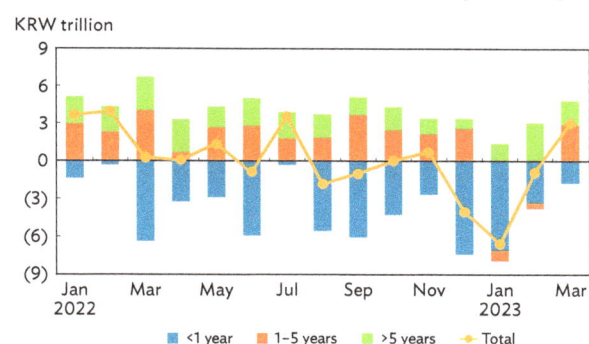

Figure 7: Net Foreign Investment in Local Currency Bonds in the Republic of Korea by Remaining Maturity

KRW = Korean won.
Source: Financial Supervisory Service.

# Malaysia

## Yield Movements

**The local currency (LCY) government bond yield curve of Malaysia flattened between 1 March and 2 June (Figure 1).** The movement of the yield curve of Malaysian fixed-income securities largely tracked the movement of the yield curve of United States (US) Treasury bonds, wherein short-term yields increased while long-term yields fell. Malaysian LCY government bonds benefited from the renewed attractiveness of emerging markets as the US Federal Reserve signaled that it would soon halt its interest rate hikes. On 9 March, Bank Negara Malaysia decided to keep its overnight policy rate unchanged amid strong economic growth in 2022 and moderating but still elevated consumer price inflation. The Malaysian central bank had a surprise rate hike on 3 May, increasing the overnight policy rate by 25 basis points to 3.00%, as a precautionary measure against potential financial risks.

### Figure 2: Composition of Local Currency Bonds Outstanding in Malaysia

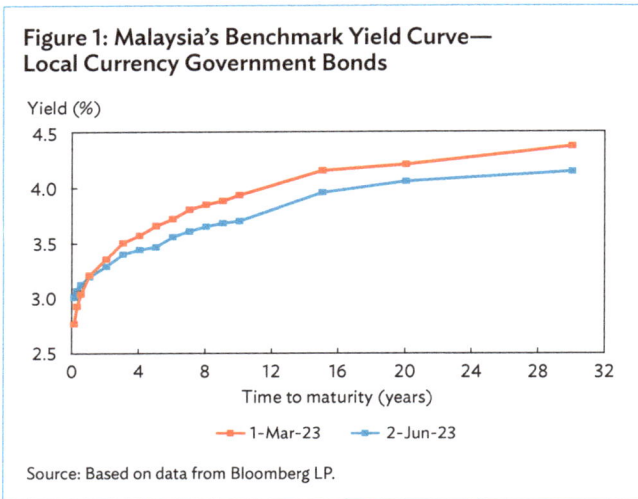

LCY = local currency, LHS = left-hand side, MYR = Malaysian ringgit, q-o-q = quarter-on-quarter, RHS = right-hand side.
Source: Bank Negara Malaysia Fully Automated System for Issuing/Tendering.

### Figure 1: Malaysia's Benchmark Yield Curve— Local Currency Government Bonds

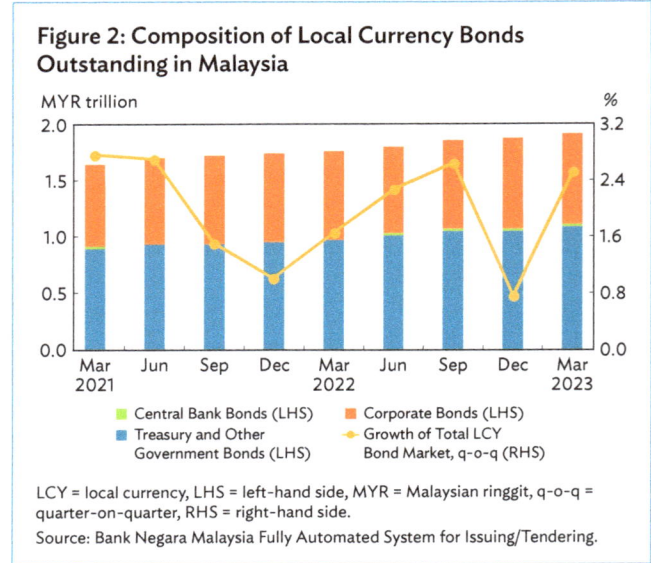

Source: Based on data from Bloomberg LP.

## Local Currency Bond Market Size and Issuance

**The Malaysian LCY bond market expanded 2.5% quarter-on-quarter (q-o-q) in the first quarter (Q1) of 2023, reaching MYR1.9 trillion (USD433.5 billion) at the end of March; growth was hindered somewhat by declining maturities (Figure 2).** This extended the growth of 0.8% q-o-q posted in the previous quarter, with an expansion in all outstanding LCY bond types contributing to the Q1 2023 growth. Outstanding Treasury and other government securities increased at a faster pace than in the fourth quarter (Q4) of 2022, continuing to be the main drivers of growth in the Malaysian LCY bond market. Outstanding fixed-income securities of the Government of Malaysia constituted a majority of the LCY bond market. Meanwhile, growth in Bank Negara Malaysia bills outstanding rebounded from Q4 2022. Corporate bonds outstanding also expanded in Q1 2023, but at a slower pace than in the prior quarter as issuers reduced their issuance amid uncertainties in global financial markets due to the turmoil in the banking industry in the US. Government-owned finance company DanaInfra Nasional continued to top all corporate bond issuers with total outstanding LCY bonds worth MYR82.3 billion at the end of March 2023.

**Malaysian LCY bond issuance contracted 14.4% q-o-q in Q1 2023 due to a decline in the issuance of LCY corporate bonds (Figure 3).** Aside from uncertainties in the financial market, the reduced issuance of LCY corporate bonds in Q1 2023 was also the result of a high base from the previous quarter. This offset the rebound in issuance of Treasury and other government bonds and central bank bills. Malaysian Government Securities (conventional bonds) and Government Investment Issues (*sukuk* or Islamic bonds) drove the 54.4% q-o-q growth in Treasury and other government bonds. During the

**Figure 3: Composition of Local Currency Bond Issuance in Malaysia**

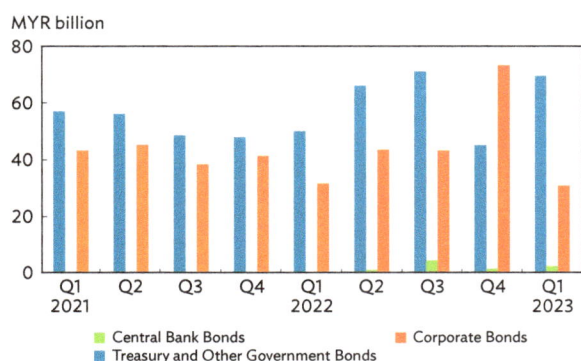

MYR = Malaysian ringgit, Q1 = first quarter, Q2 = second quarter, Q3 = third quarter, Q4 = fourth quarter.
Source: Bank Negara Malaysia Fully Automated System for Issuing/Tendering.

**Figure 4: Composition of Local Currency Islamic Bonds Outstanding in Malaysia**

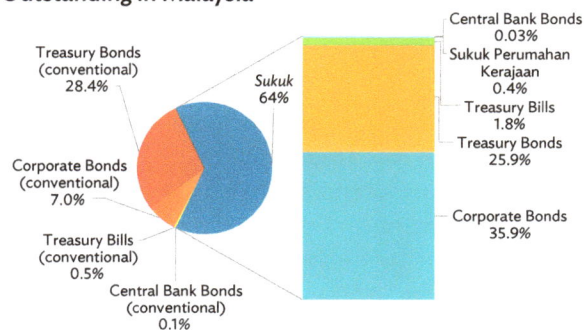

MYR = Malaysian ringgit.
Note: Sukuk Perumahan Kerajaan are Islamic bonds issued by the Government of Malaysia to refinance funding for housing loans to government employees and to extend new housing loans.
Source: Bank Negara Malaysia Fully Automated System for Issuing/Tendering.

review period, Maybank Islamic had the largest aggregate issuance with eight Islamic commercial paper issuances totaling MYR4.0 billion.

**Outstanding *sukuk* comprised 64.0% of Malaysia's LCY bond market in Q1 2023 (Figure 4).** Islamic bonds outstanding amounted to MYR1.2 trillion at the end of March, growing 3.6% q-o-q. Outstanding corporate *sukuk* continued to drive the Islamic bond market as they comprised a majority of LCY corporate bonds outstanding at the end of Q1 2023.

## Capital Flows

**Capital inflows worth MYR13.0 billion were recorded in Q1 2023 (Figure 5).** Foreign investors turned to emerging markets after the Federal Reserve signaled that it would soon halt its interest rate hikes. Foreign holdings of LCY government bonds slightly increased to 22.7% at the end of March from 22.4% at the end of December.

**Figure 5: Capital Flows in the Malaysian Local Currency Government Bond Market**

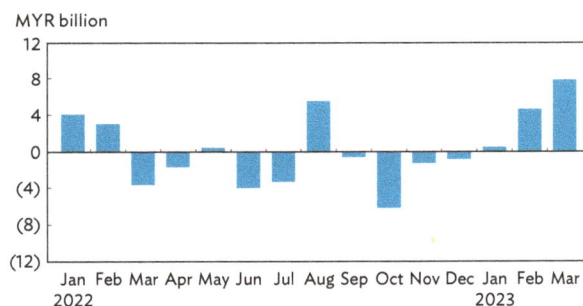

( ) = negative, MYR = Malaysian ringgit.
Notes:
1. Figures exclude foreign holdings of central bank bonds.
2. Month-on-month changes in foreign holdings of local currency government bonds were used as a proxy for bond flows.
Source: Bank Negara Malaysia Monthly Statistical Bulletin.

# Philippines

## Yield Movements

**The local currency (LCY) government bond yield curve of the Philippines rose for shorter tenors and shifted downward for longer tenors between 1 March and 2 June (Figure 1).** The increase in yields at the short-end of the curve was in line with the Bangko Sentral ng Pilipinas' (BSP) monetary tightening, with a total increase of 425 basis points (bps) from nine rate hikes between May 2022 and March 2023. On the other hand, the decline in yields at the longer end was influenced by expectations of a slowdown in domestic inflation. This allowed the BSP to moderate the pace of its rate hike by 25 bps in its 23 March policy meeting before holding rates steady at 6.25% on 18 May. On a year-on-year basis, consumer price inflation eased further to 6.1% in May from 6.6% in April, 7.6% in March, and 8.6% in February. In addition, the falling yields at the longer end were influenced by market expectations of the United States Federal Reserve's rate-hike cycle nearing its end.

## Local Currency Bond Market Size and Issuance

**The outstanding amount of LCY bonds in the Philippines grew 3.1% quarter-on-quarter (q-o-q) to PHP11.5 trillion (USD212.4 billion) in the first quarter (Q1) of 2023.** The LCY q-o-q growth was driven by an expansion of government bonds amid increased issuances driven by the government's frontloading policy. On the

other hand, corporate bonds contracted 2.2% q-o-q as maturities exceeded issuances in Q1 2023. Treasury and other government bonds remained dominant in the Philippines' LCY bond market, accounting for 81.6% of the total debt stock at the end of March, while corporate bonds and central bank securities accounted for 13.6% and 4.8%, respectively (**Figure 2**). Banking, property, and holding firms were the three sectors that dominated the Philippine corporate bond market, accounting for a collective share of 80.6% of total corporate bonds outstanding at the end of March 2023 (**Figure 3**).

**Figure 2: Composition of Local Currency Bonds Outstanding in the Philippines**

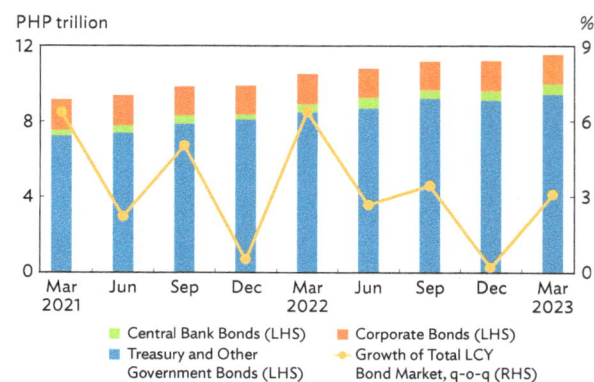

Central Bank Bonds (LHS)
Corporate Bonds (LHS)
Treasury and Other Government Bonds (LHS)
Growth of Total LCY Bond Market, q-o-q (RHS)

LCY = local currency, LHS = left-hand side, PHP = Philippine peso, q-o-q = quarter-on-quarter, RHS = right-hand side.

Note: Treasury and other government bonds comprise Treasury bonds, Treasury bills, and bonds issued by government agencies, entities, and corporations for which repayment is guaranteed by the Government of the Philippines. This includes bonds issued by Power Sector Assets and Liabilities Management and the National Food Authority, among others.

Source: Bureau of the Treasury and Bloomberg LP.

**Figure 1: The Philippines' Benchmark Yield Curve—Local Currency Government Bonds**

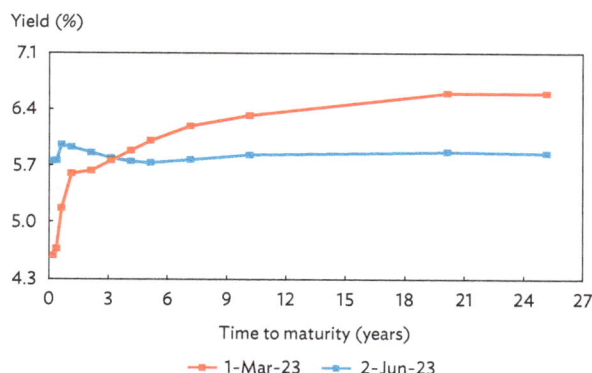

1-Mar-23
2-Jun-23

Source: Based on data from Bloomberg LP.

**Figure 3: Local Currency Corporate Bonds Outstanding by Sector**

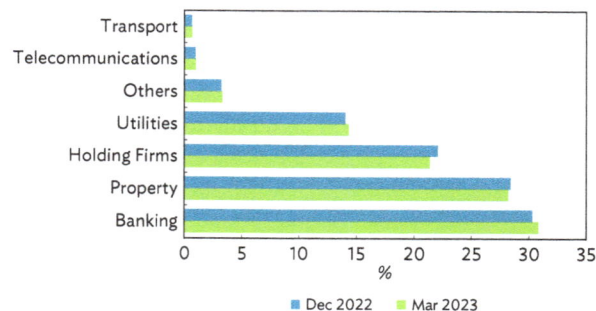

Transport
Telecommunications
Others
Utilities
Holding Firms
Property
Banking

Dec 2022
Mar 2023

Source: Bureau of the Treasury.

Among corporate issuers, only property firms and holding firms posted a q-o-q decline in their respective market shares during the quarter. The transport and telecommunications sectors remained the smallest issuers of corporate bonds with marginal market shares of less than 1.0% each at the end of Q1 2023.

**The Philippines' total LCY bond issuance in Q1 2023 expanded 24.7% q-o-q to reach PHP2.7 trillion, buoyed by the government's issuance of Retail Treasury Bonds (RTBs) in February.** RTBs were issued by the Government of the Philippines carrying a tenor of 5.5 years and a 6.125% coupon rate (with exchange offer). Through this offering, the government raised PHP283.7 billion, of which PHP162.2 billion was awarded at the rate-setting auction and an additional PHP121.5 billion was raised during the 1-week offer period (PHP89.9 billion via new money and PHP31.7 billion through a bond exchange). Treasury and other government bonds accounted for 34.8% of all LCY bonds issued during the quarter. In contrast, corporate bond issuance contracted 81.7% q-o-q in Q1 2023 amid higher interest rates (**Figure 4**). Corporate bond issuance reached PHP23.3 billion during the quarter and comprised a 0.9% share of the issuance total. Central bank securities comprised the largest share of fixed-income securities issuance in the Philippine LCY bond market in Q1 2023, accounting for 64.3% of the total quarterly issuance volume.

## Investor Profile

**Nearly half of the total LCY government debt stock was held by banks and investment houses at the end of March (Figure 5).** Banks and investment houses comprise the only investor group that posted a q-o-q increase in its holdings share in Q1 2023, rising to 46.4% from 44.0% in the previous quarter. The holdings share of contractual savings institutions and tax-exempt institutions, the second-largest investor group in the Philippine LCY government bond market, slightly decreased to 32.0% in Q1 2023 from 33.5% in the previous quarter. Government-owned or -controlled corporations remained the smallest investor group with a holdings share of less than 1.0% at the end of March.

**Figure 5: Investor Profile of Local Currency Government Bonds**

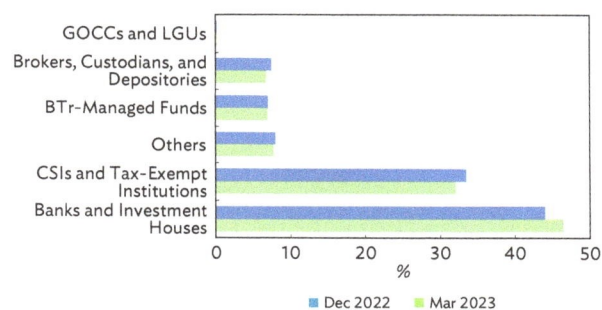

BTr = Bureau of the Treasury, CSI = contractual savings institution, GOCC = government-owned or -controlled corporation, LGU = local government unit.
Source: Bureau of the Treasury.

**Figure 4: Composition of Local Currency Bond Issuance in the Philippines**

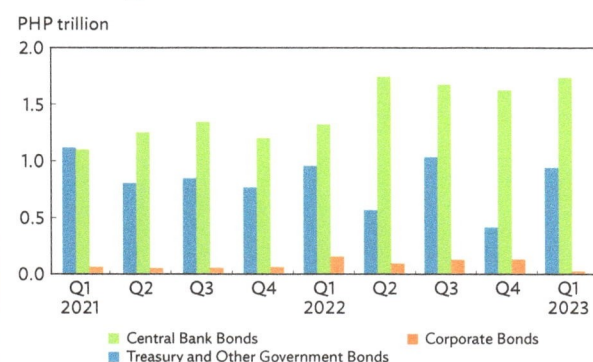

Q1 = first quarter, Q2 = second quarter, Q3 = third quarter, Q4 = fourth quarter, PHP = Philippine peso.
Note: Treasury and other government bonds comprise Treasury bonds, Treasury bills, and bonds issued by government agencies, entities, and corporations for which repayment is guaranteed by the Government of the Philippines. This includes bonds issued by Power Sector Assets and Liabilities Management and the National Food Authority, among others.
Sources: Bureau of the Treasury and Bloomberg LP.

# Singapore

## Yield Movements

The local currency (LCY) government bond yields of Singapore declined for all tenors, except the 3-month yield, between 1 March and 2 June (**Figure 1**). Investors remained concerned about long-term financial conditions due to uncertainties in the path of monetary tightening in the United States. On 14 April, the Monetary Authority of Singapore (MAS) decided to keep the rate of appreciation of its Singapore dollar nominal effective exchange rate steady amid the appreciation of the Singapore dollar since its last monetary policy

tightening on 14 October 2022 (**Figure 2**). Tepid economic growth and declining consumer price inflation prompted the Singapore central bank to keep its monetary policy unchanged.

## Local Currency Bond Market Size and Issuance

The Singapore LCY bond market expanded 1.3% quarter-on-quarter (q-o-q) to SGD670.3 billion (USD503.7 billion) in the first quarter (Q1) of 2023, supported by increased central bank securities outstanding. MAS securities extended their growth to 4.2% q-o-q from the 3.8% q-o-q expansion posted in the prior quarter. MAS bills continued to comprise the largest chunk of Singapore's LCY bond market during the review period as the central bank uses these securities to manage liquidity in Singapore's financial market (**Figure 3**). The LCY bond market's growth at the end of March, however, was hampered by the decline in Singapore Government Securities bills and bonds and LCY corporate bonds outstanding of 0.4% q-o-q and 0.5% q-o-q, respectively. These contractions were a reversal from the growth of 1.8% q-o-q and 1.2% q-o-q, respectively, recorded in the fourth quarter (Q4) of 2022. Government-owned Housing & Development Board continued to top all issuers with SGD28.2 billion worth of outstanding bonds at the end of March 2023.

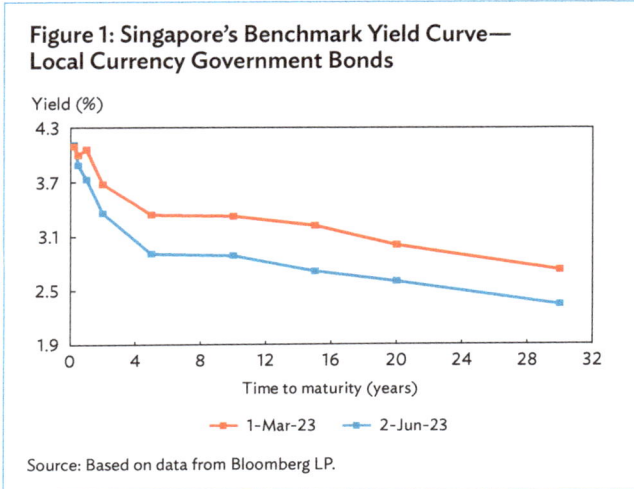

**Figure 1: Singapore's Benchmark Yield Curve— Local Currency Government Bonds**

Source: Based on data from Bloomberg LP.

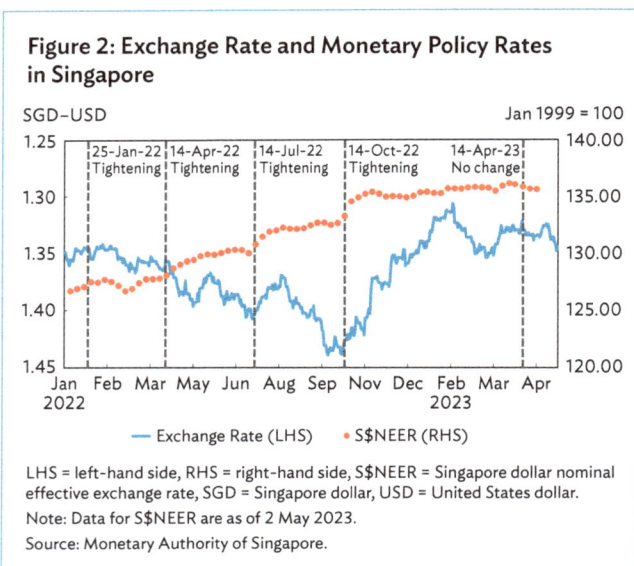

**Figure 2: Exchange Rate and Monetary Policy Rates in Singapore**

LHS = left-hand side, RHS = right-hand side, S$NEER = Singapore dollar nominal effective exchange rate, SGD = Singapore dollar, USD = United States dollar.
Note: Data for S$NEER are as of 2 May 2023.
Source: Monetary Authority of Singapore.

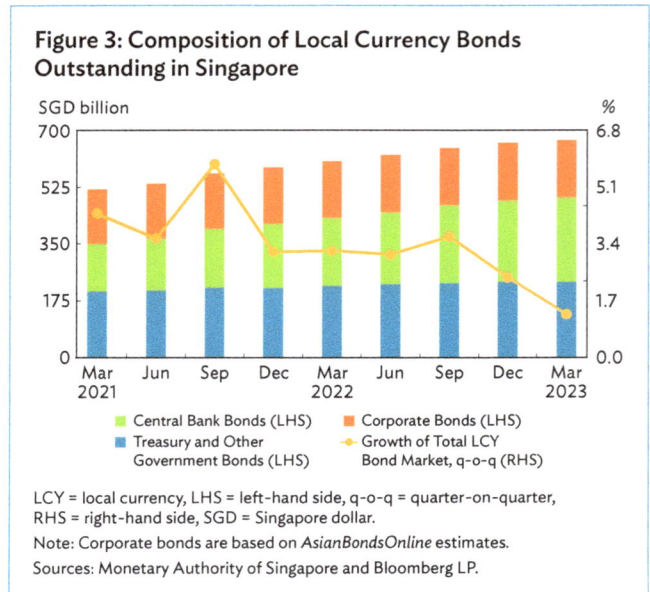

**Figure 3: Composition of Local Currency Bonds Outstanding in Singapore**

LCY = local currency, LHS = left-hand side, q-o-q = quarter-on-quarter, RHS = right-hand side, SGD = Singapore dollar.
Note: Corporate bonds are based on *AsianBondsOnline* estimates.
Sources: Monetary Authority of Singapore and Bloomberg LP.

Singapore's total LCY bond issuance rebounded in Q1 2023, expanding 5.0% q-o-q as issuance in all bond segments rebounded (**Figure 4**). MAS securities continued to dominate LCY bond issuance during the quarter. The bills are regularly offered by the Government of Singapore for liquidity management. LCY corporate bond issuance increased in Q1 2023 but remained tepid amid uncertainties in global financial markets spurred by the turmoil in the banking industry in the United States. Despite this, United Overseas Bank raised SGD850.0 million from a perpetual bond issuance in January. The issuance was the largest corporate issue during the quarter, with the fixed-income security also qualifying as part of the bank's additional tier 1 capital.

**Figure 4: Composition of Local Currency Bond Issuance in Singapore**

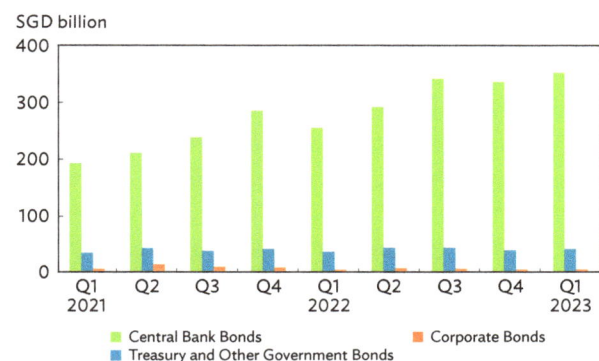

Q1 = first quarter, Q2 = second quarter, Q3 = third quarter, Q4 = fourth quarter, SGD = Singapore dollar.

Note: Corporate bonds are based on *AsianBondsOnline* estimates.

Sources: Monetary Authority of Singapore and Bloomberg LP.

# Thailand

## Yield Movements

**Between 1 March and 2 June, Thailand's local currency (LCY) government bond yield curve flattened, with yields rising at the shorter end but falling for all tenors longer than 4 years (Figure 1).** The flattening of the yield curve reflected elevated short-term uncertainties following the general election in May. Bank of Thailand's (BOT) policy rate hikes also drove the rise at the shorter-end of the yield curve. The BOT has been among the more aggressive central banks in the region this year in the fight against inflation. To keep inflation in check, the BOT raised its benchmark rate by 25 basis points each during its 25 January, 29 March, and 31 May meetings, bringing the key rate to 2.00%. Consumer price inflation has been on a downward trend since January, with the April reading of 2.7% year-on-year (y-o-y) falling within the BOT's target range of 1.0% to 3.0%. Nonetheless, the central bank noted that core inflation remained elevated and increased demand amid economic recovery and possible higher spending by the new government could create additional upward pressure on prices. Meanwhile, the decline in yields of most mid-to long-term bonds followed regional yield movements, which trended down on expectations that the United States Federal Reserve would pause its monetary policy tightening during its June meeting.

## Local Currency Bond Market Size and Issuance

**Thailand's LCY bond market continued to expand, reaching a size of THB15.9 trillion (USD466.4 billion) at the end of March.** Growth picked up by 2.1% quarter-on-quarter (q-o-q) in the first quarter (Q1) of 2023 from 0.8% q-o-q in the previous quarter, driven primarily by rapid expansion in the corporate bond market amid continued economic recovery. Thailand's gross domestic product growth accelerated to 2.7% y-o-y in Q1 2023, driven by the sustained resurgence of domestic demand and tourism. Growth in Treasury and other government bonds also contributed to the overall LCY bond market expansion. With an outstanding stock of THB9.0 trillion, Treasury and other government bonds accounted for 56.5% of the total LCY bond market (**Figure 2**). Outstanding corporate bonds (THB4.6 trillion) and BOT bonds (THB2.3 trillion) comprised the remaining shares of 28.9% and 14.6%, respectively.

### Figure 1: Thailand's Benchmark Yield Curve— Local Currency Government Bonds

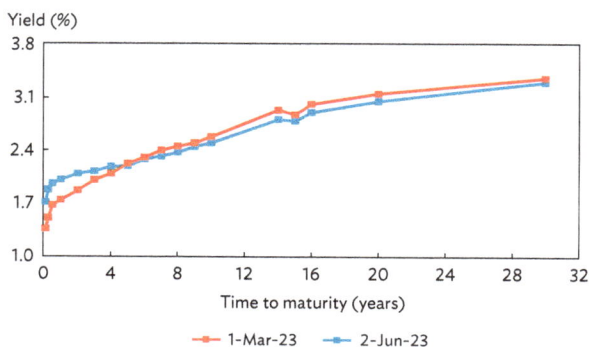

Source: Based on data from Bloomberg LP.

### Figure 2: Composition of Local Currency Bonds Outstanding in Thailand

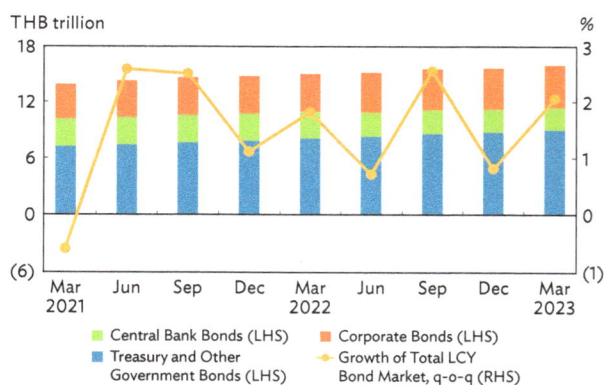

( ) = negative, LCY = local currency, LHS = left-hand side, q-o-q = quarter-on-quarter, RHS = right-hand side, THB = Thai baht.
Source: Bank of Thailand.

**LCY bond issuance tallied THB2.3 trillion in Q1 2023, driven by a rebound in corporate bond issuance.** New issuances of LCY bonds rose 5.1% q-o-q in Q1 2023, reversing the 0.3% q-o-q contraction posted in the previous quarter (**Figure 3**). Growth stemmed primarily from corporate bond issuance, which rose 10.2% q-o-q in Q1 2023 following a 10.9% q-o-q decline in the preceding quarter. Total issuance of new corporate debt reached THB546.9 billion in Q1 2023. The rebound in corporate bond issuance was influenced by improved investor confidence amid sustained economic recovery. The largest corporate issuer in Q1 2023 was True Corporation with a total issuance volume of THB20.8 billion. Meanwhile, issuance of Treasury and other government bonds totaled THB608.1 billion, down 1.7% q-o-q in Q1 2023. The decline in Treasury issuance was mainly due to a high base as the previous quarter saw a record issuance of THB46.1 billion of savings bonds.

## Investor Profile

**Insurance and pension funds remained the primary holders of Thailand's LCY government bonds.** Nonetheless, their share of LCY government bond holdings slipped to 45.9% at the end of March 2023 from 46.9% a year earlier (**Figure 4**). Foreign holdings also eased to 12.3% from 13.7% during the same period. In contrast, the BOT's holdings of LCY government bonds rose to 6.4% at the end of March from 4.2% a year prior. To help stabilize the government bond market, the BOT purchased a total of THB85.7 billion of government bonds between March 2022 and March 2023.

**Figure 4: Investor Profile of Government Bonds in Thailand**

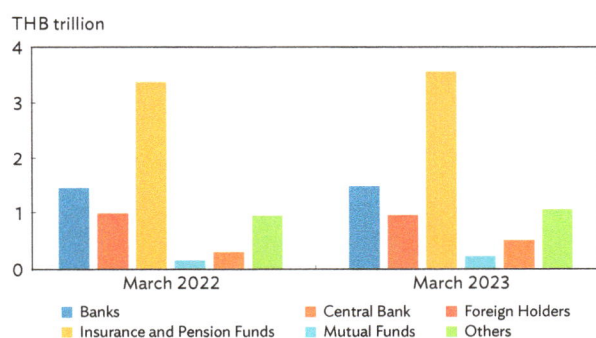

THB trillion

| | March 2022 | March 2023 |
| --- | --- | --- |

Banks  Central Bank  Foreign Holders
Insurance and Pension Funds  Mutual Funds  Others

THB = Thai baht.
Source: Bank of Thailand.

**Figure 3: Composition of Local Currency Bond Issuance in Thailand**

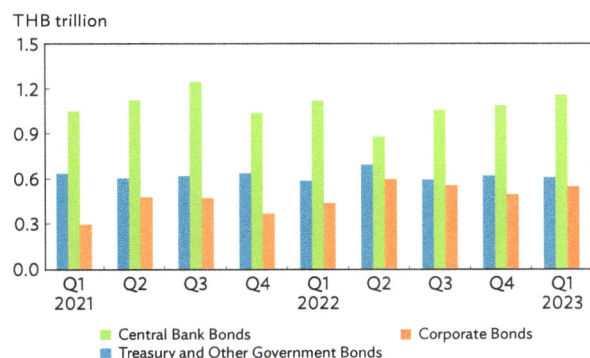

THB trillion

Q1 2021, Q2, Q3, Q4, Q1 2022, Q2, Q3, Q4, Q1 2023

Central Bank Bonds  Corporate Bonds
Treasury and Other Government Bonds

Q1 = first quarter, Q2 = second quarter, Q3 = third quarter, Q4 = fourth quarter, THB = Thai baht.
Source: Bank of Thailand.

# Viet Nam

## Yield Movements

**Viet Nam's local currency (LCY) government bond yields declined for all maturities between 1 March and 2 June (Figure 1).** Declining yields were mainly driven by the State Bank of Vietnam's (SBV) monetary easing stance, as it reduced the refinancing rate by 50 basis points (bps) each in its meetings on 31 March and 23 May, bringing the main policy rate to 5.00%. Prior to this, in its 14 March meeting, the SBV lowered the discount rate and overnight lending rate by 100 bps. The rate cuts were taken to spur economic growth amid cooling inflation. In May, Viet Nam's year-on-year (y-o-y) consumer price inflation decelerated to 2.4% from 2.8% in April, while Viet Nam's economic growth slowed to 3.3% y-o-y in the first quarter (Q1) of 2023 from 5.9% y-o-y in the fourth quarter of 2022. As inflation continues to be under the government's target of 4.5%, and the United States (US) Federal Reserve moves toward a dovish monetary stance, SBV is keeping its monetary policy flexible with room for further rate cuts to support Viet Nam's economic growth and foster financial stability especially in the real estate industry. The SBV further reduced by 50 bps the refinancing rate (4.50%), rediscount rate (3.00%), and overnight lending rate (5.00%) on 16 June.

## Local Currency Bond Market Size and Issuance

**The LCY bond market in Viet Nam grew 5.1% quarter-on-quarter (q-o-q) to reach a size of VND2,626.1 trillion (USD111.9 billion) at the end of March.** Growth can be attributed to expansions in both the government and corporate bond segments amid increased issuance during the quarter. Corporate bond market growth rebounded as the government eased some regulations, leading to the resurgence of issuance during the quarter. At the end of March, Viet Nam's LCY bond market remained dominated by Treasury and other government bonds, which together accounted for 67.8% of the total bonds outstanding, while a 28.0% share was attributable to corporate bonds and a 4.2% share was attributable to central bank securities (**Figure 2**). Financial institutions and property firms are the largest issuers of corporate bonds in Viet Nam's LCY corporate bond market, accounting for 53.8% and 25.5%, respectively, of the total corporate bond stock at the end of March.

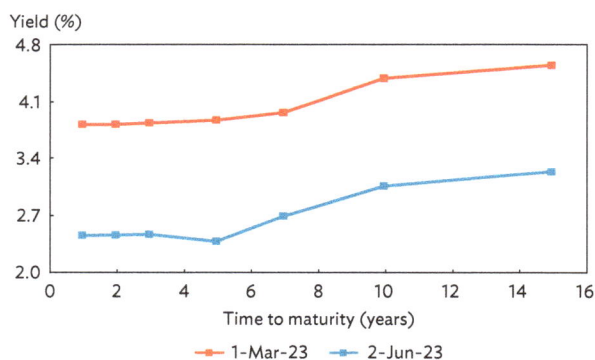

**Figure 1: Viet Nam's Benchmark Yield Curve—Local Currency Government Bonds**

Source: Based on data from Bloomberg LP.

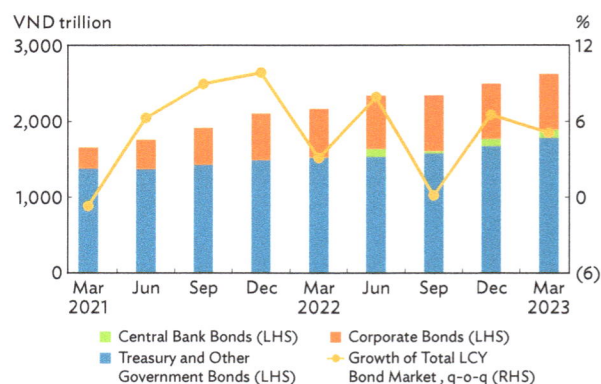

**Figure 2: Composition of Local Currency Bonds Outstanding in Viet Nam**

LCY = local currency, LHS = left-hand side, q-o-q = quarter-on-quarter, RHS = right-hand side, VND = Vietnamese dong.
Note: Other government bonds comprise government-guaranteed and municipal bonds.
Sources: Vietnam Bond Market Association and Bloomberg LP.

**LCY bond issuance in Viet Nam climbed 73.0% q-o-q in Q1 2023 to reach VND938.4 trillion.** Issuance of Treasury and other government bonds grew 15.9% q-o-q to VND121.4 trillion in Q1 2023, from VND104.8 trillion in the fourth quarter of 2022, accounting for 12.9% of the issuance total during the quarter. Issuance of corporate bonds expanded significantly in Q1 2023 (639.3% q-o-q), as activity in the corporate bond market picked up following the government's issuance of Decree No. 8 in March, after which 93.0% of the quarter's corporate bond issuance occurred.[7] Furthermore, 85.3% of the corporate issuances in Q1 2023 were issued by seven firms in the property sector. Decree No. 8 was issued amid a slow recovery in Viet Nam's corporate bond market due to the government's credit tightening policies, high interest rates, and declining bond issuance volumes, which stifled bond issuers' funding sources and hampered their ability to meet their bond obligations. Based on the FiinRatings report released in April, total default value of corporate bonds reached VND94.4 trillion as of 17 March from 69 issuer companies. The real estate industry accounted for the largest share of 83.6% (VND78.9 trillion) of

the total default value. Defaulted bonds continued to increase to a total of VND128.5 trillion as of 4 May. During the quarter, total corporate bond issuance reached VND28.4 trillion, equivalent to 3.0% of the total LCY issued bonds in Q1 2023 (**Figure 3**). Hung Yen Investment and Development, a company engaged in real estate business, was the largest corporate bond issuer during the quarter, with aggregate issuance of VND7.2 trillion. Meanwhile, central bank securities comprised the largest share of issuance volume in the overall LCY bond market, accounting for 84.0% of the issuance total in Q1 2023.

## Investor Profile

**The combined holdings of insurance companies and banks continued to account for nearly all outstanding LCY government bonds in Viet Nam at the end of March** (**Figure 4**). Insurance companies remained the largest investor group with an investment share of 57.8% by the end of Q1 2023, a slight decline from 58.9% in the previous quarter. Meanwhile, banks' holdings of government bonds increased to 41.7% at the end of March. Security companies and investment funds, as well as offshore investors, continued to hold a marginal share of less than 1.0% each at the end of March 2023.

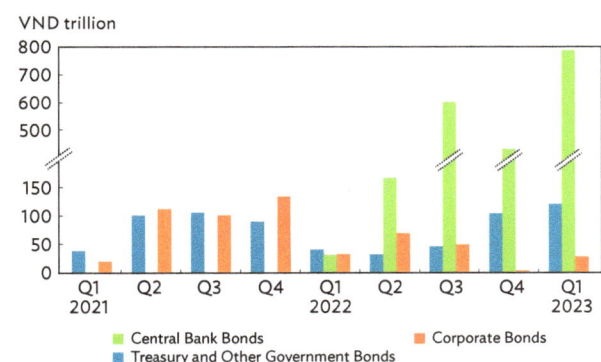

**Figure 3: Composition of Local Currency Bond Issuance in Viet Nam**

Q1 = first quarter, Q2 = second quarter, Q3 = third quarter, Q4 = fourth quarter, VND = Vietnamese dong.
Note: Other government bonds comprise government-guaranteed and municipal bonds.
Sources: Vietnam Bond Market Association and Bloomberg LP.

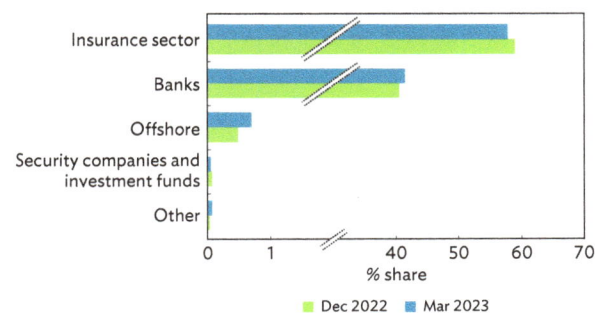

**Figure 4: Investor Profile of Local Currency Government Bonds**

Source: Vietnam Ministry of Finance.

---

[7] Decree No. 8 issued by the government on 5 March eased corporate bond regulations by amending the following provisions previously stipulated in Decree No. 65: (i) payment by assets other than cash is now accepted for domestically issued bonds; (ii) issuers can extend payments by a maximum of 2 years if holders agree, and; (iii) requirements for professional investor status, credit ratings, and the rule on 30-day distribution period for each private placement are now postponed to 1 January 2024.